# *Historic Tales*

### *of*

# MEIGS COUNTY
## OHIO

# *Historic Tales*
## *of*
# MEIGS COUNTY
## OHIO

JORDAN D. PICKENS &
CALEE M. PICKENS

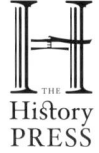

THE
History
PRESS

Published by The History Press
Charleston, SC
www.historypress.com

First published 2019

Manufactured in the United States

ISBN 9781467144254

Library of Congress Control Number: 2019950037

*We dedicate this book to anyone who has ever called Meigs County home.*

*—Jordan and Calee Pickens*

* ❈ *

*To Andrew and Clara, all our love,*

*—Dad and Mom*

# CONTENTS

# CONTENTS

# Chapter 1

# MEIGS COUNTY'S TOWNSHIPS

M eigs County was created on April 1, 1819, from parts of Athens and Gallia Counties, though originally Washington County included all of what would become Gallia, Athens and Meigs Counties. Gallia County was organized in 1803, and Athens County was formed in 1805. The interesting township history of these counties before the creation of Meigs County is often overlooked.

In 1803, Letart Township was organized as one of the three townships that made up Gallia County, and by 1810, it had a population of 501. Letart Township's original boundaries stretched from the mouth of the Shade River, followed the Ohio River to Kerr's Run, then turned north to the county line and finally returned east to meet the mouth of the Shade River. The area encompassed all of present-day Sutton and Lebanon Townships, as well as parts of Orange and Olive Townships. According to *Ervin's Pioneer History of Meigs County*, "Tradition has it that on the Falls at Letart the body of a Frenchman was found drowned in the Ohio River and on his arm was tattooed the name 'Letart.'" Various history books and maps have reported this area as Tart's Falls, Le Tart, Let' Art and Letartsville.

Salisbury Township was organized in 1805 as part of Gallia County. Part of the original Salisbury territory extended west to present-day Ross County. In the shifting of the of the territory in its first year of establishment, part of it was known as Kerr Township—named for Hamilton Kerr, one of the early settlers where Kerr's Run is today. In 1807, Salisbury Township was reorganized to its present boundaries, and from its old boundaries, Rutland

Township (1812) and Salem Township (1813) were created. Salisbury Township is believed to have gotten its name from Salisbury, England, in Wiltshire County, which was settled at the confluence of the Avon, Nadder, Ebble, Wylye and Bourne Rivers. Salisbury Township was similarly laid out where Kerr's Run, Naylor's Run, Sugar Run, Africa Run (now Monkey Run), Leading Creek and Story's Run all meet at the Ohio River.

Rutland Township, named for Rutland, Massachusetts, home of General Rufus Putnam, was organized in 1812. Rutland, Massachusetts, was named in honor of the Duke of Rutland of England in 1686. When Rutland Township was originally surveyed, it was 36 square miles. When it was decided to organize Meigs County, there was fear that the area set aside would not meet the minimum 400–420 square miles required to form a county. To alleviate this problem, in April 1819, an additional row of twelve sections were taken from Gallia County (six from Morgan Township and six from Cheshire Township) and given to Meigs County (six in Salem Township and six in Rutland Township).

Lebanon Township was organized in 1813 from Letart Township. Lebanon Township boasts the largest span of Ohio River frontage, with a total of fourteen and a half miles. The township earned the name Lebanon because of its dense forests at the time of its founding. In the Bible, the cedar of Lebanon is mentioned seventy-seven times.

According to *Larkin's Pioneer History of Meigs County*,

> [Lebanon] was a dense forest at the time of its organization. Trees of great size, and timber of the finest quality, covered the rich bottom lands of the Ohio River and the creeks of Old Town and Groundhog, while the hills bore the best yellow pine and spruce for lumber. The sugar maple, hickory, black oak and white oak, poplar, beech and sycamore trees excelled any forests in Europe in size and quality of lumber. The black walnut, white walnut and wild cherry were favorite woods for the manufacture of furniture, and for inside work of the best houses. Black walnut and cherry were used particularly for the making of coffins in those early days. So, these trees of Lebanon had special attractions to the commercial eyes of later emigrants.

Salem Township, which originally included present-day Vinton County's Wilkesville Township, was set off from Salisbury Township in 1814. It is one of fourteen townships in Ohio to bear the name Salem, after Salem, Massachusetts, home to many of the members of the Ohio

Company of Associates, which purchased this land. The first settler of the eventual Salem Township was Captain James Merrill, a seafaring man who commanded vessels owned by Timothy Dexter in the East India Trade. After years of service, Dexter, weary of sea life, gave Merrill a farm and large tract of land from his share of the Ohio Company purchase, with the intention of having Merrill settle the land and take charge of the remainder. Merrill built the first frame house in present-day Meigs County. Merrill named Dexter Creek after his former employer, paying homage to Dexter's business on water. Since Dexter Creek was named first, the town of Dexter was actually named after the creek. A year after Salem Township was settled, Wilkesville organized as a separate township.

Sutton Township was organized in 1814 from part of Letart Township and was established by the Gallia County commissioners on October 21, 1817. Dr. Fuller Elliot suggested the name to the commissioners as a way of honoring his native New England town of Sutton, Massachusetts. The first post office was established at Graham Station (now Racine) in 1818, and Andrew Donnally was appointed as the first postmaster. Early on, Sutton Township's villages were Graham Station, Minersville, Syracuse and Careltonville.

Orange Township was organized in 1813 as part of Athens County and is the most peculiarly named of all of Meigs County's townships. Orange Township is only 25.8 square miles and is the second-smallest township in Meigs County, behind Letart Township. Orange Township encompassed nearly all of Olive Township—most of what is now Chester Township—until March 1, 1824, and part of Troy Township in Athens County. The township received its name from Orange Borrows—one of the three sons of George Borrows, who came to what is now Canaan Township in Athens County in 1797. Tuppers Plains, which is on the border with Olive Township and gets its name from Benjamin Tupper, was laid out in 1840 by James Martin. Alfred, Orange Township's only other municipality, was laid out in 1874 by Peter Hoffman. There are six Orange Townships in Ohio.

The following is from *Larkin's Pioneer History of Meigs County*:

> Proceedings approved by the Court of Common Pleas, July 24th, 1819. The board adjourned until the twenty-first of July, 1819. An application was made this day to divide the township of Orange. Resolved, that said township of Orange [is to] be divided as follows: Beginning on the Ohio River at the southeast corner of Section 29, Township 3, Range 11, west to the northwest corner of Section No. 5, Township 3, Range

12; thence north to the county line; thence east with said line to the Ohio River; thence with the meanderings of said river to the place of beginning; and that the name of the township be Olive.

Olive Township is named after Olive Reed, son of Major Reed (the gentleman's name, not referring to his rank in military service), who moved to the area in 1816, after living in Belpre for only a year after serving his country. Major Reed laid out Randolph's Landing in 1855. The name "Randolph's Landing" comes from ferryboat owner and captain Joseph Randolph. The name of the post office, and eventually the community, was changed to Reedville (for Major Reed's brothers Samuel and Willard) on May 27, 1863, when Thomas C. Hardman became postmaster. Over the years, the possessive *s* was added to make the name Reedsville. Reedsville is one of the highest points of elevation on the Ohio River between Pittsburgh and Cincinnati and was nicknamed "Cooper Shop Town" due to the many barrels that were manufactured there. Long Bottom was laid out in 1866 by Daniel McKee, taking its name from the long stretch of bottomland extending along the river above the present community.

Bedford Township was organized on June 22, 1821, and is said to be named in honor of New Bedford, Massachusetts, because of settlers from the Ohio Company of Associates, although it is possible that it is named after Bedford County, Pennsylvania. The first settlers of Bedford Township were Leroy Jones, Warren Bissel, William Cook (Cook Road's namesake), Firman Couch and Harland Kingsbury (brother-in-law to Levi Stedman). In 1806, Harland Kingsbury built the first cabin at the first fork of the West Branch of the Shade River, now known as Kingsbury Creek. In its early history, Bedford Township was said to have many apple, peach and plum orchards and three distilleries. The first sawmill was built on Kingsbury Creek in 1828 by Alden Bissill. There is only one other Bedford Township in Ohio, located in Coshocton County. The name Burlingham is a bastardization of the name Burlingame, one of the pioneer families who settled in the township. Burlingham allegedly received the nickname of "Bungtown" in the late 1800s when several local women got upset with their husbands for spending too much time at the local saloon. They are said to have knocked all of the bungs (similar to a cork stopper) out of the whiskey barrels and used the escaping liquor to burn down the saloon.

Scipio Township was part of Athens County prior to the formation of Meigs County in 1819, and its earliest settlement was made by Jeremiah Riggs in 1799, where Pageville is now situated. Pageville was originally called

Downington Post Office, Downington for short, but was renamed for the family of Jesse Page, who came from Maine and settled in Scipio Township in 1816. Pageville was laid out in 1838 by Amos Stevens. Harrisonville was laid out in 1840 by Alexander Steward and named in honor of Ohio's William Henry Harrison, who won the presidential election the same year. Scipio Township is believed to be named after Scipio, New York, which was named after Scipio Africanus, or Scipio the Great, a Roman general and later consul who is often regarded as one of the greatest generals and military strategists of all time. The village of Scipio, Ohio, is located in Butler County, and the only other Scipio Township in Ohio is in Seneca County.

Columbia Township, organized and named on April 12, 1820, was originally part of Alexander Township in Athens County. Alvin Ogdin from Columbia, Maryland, built the first log cabin in the area in 1804. Amos Carpenter Sr. came from Virginia and settled in Rutland Township, and around 1818, he sold his farm and bought a valuable tract of land in Columbia Township. It was noted in Ervin's *Pioneer History of Meigs County* that "the township was especially interested in schools and education, and a trace of one of the earliest libraries was located in this township." It's interesting to point out that Professor Will C. Meritt, born in Carpenter in 1866, went on to teach in various places in Meigs County and is said to have taught the first agriculture class in the state of Ohio. Another famous Columbia Township educator was Professor Joshua R. Morton, who went on to become a chemistry professor at Ohio University and is the namesake of Morton Hall on OU's Athens campus.

In 1822, the village of Chester was named Meigs County's seat of government. Chester Township was organized on March 1, 1824, from parts of Sutton, Salisbury and Orange Townships and was given the name at the suggestion of Colonel David Barber. Chester Township is said to be named after Chester County, Pennsylvania, one of the three original counties in the state. In 1777, Nathaniel Burrell, nicknamed the "Great Bear Hunter," settled on the middle branch of the Shade River, about one mile north of Chester Village. Chester Township is one of five with the same name in Ohio; the others are in Clinton, Geauga, Morrow and Wayne Counties.

# Chapter 2

# RUTLAND, THE HIGLEYS AND THE ROOTS OF "HOME ON THE RANGE"

*I*t's an age-old question: Which came first, the chicken or the egg? In Meigs County, the question is which came first, Rutland Village or Rutland Township? To answer the Rutland question at least, the village of Rutland was laid out in 1828, whereas Rutland Township was organized in 1812 as part of the original purchase of the Ohio Company of Associates. The name "Rutland" is also found in Vermont and Massachusetts. As General Rufus Putnam was from Rutland, Massachusetts, it is assumed Meigs County's Rutland was named after Putnam's hometown.

According to Larkin's *Pioneer History of Meigs County*,

> The first settlement made in Rutland Township was by Brewster Higley IV, in April 1799, on the farm since occupied by his son, Milo Higley. Judge Higley was a native of Simsbury, Connecticut, but came from Castleton, Rutland County, Vermont, to Bellville, West Virginia, where he remained 18 months, preparatory to his removal to Ohio. He bought a share in the Ohio Company's purchase for one thousand dollars. He then, in company with John Case, who had been one of a party of surveyors, and was of some service to Mr. Higley in making his selection of land, as he was to have a part of the land, made a visit to the place of his future home. He returned to Bellville, purchased a family boat and floated down the Ohio River to the mouth of Leading Creek, which being high with back water, he poled his boat up the

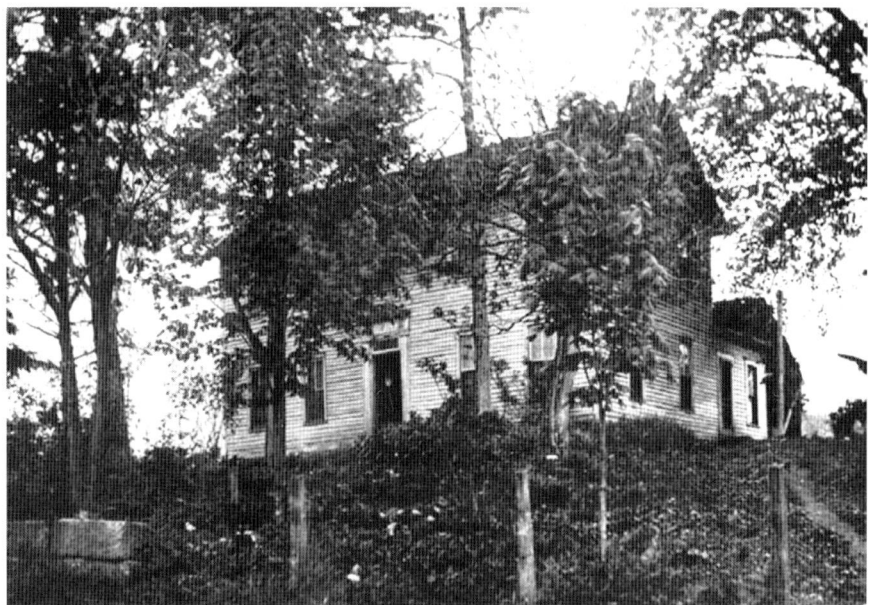

Higley family homestead. *From Kay Jenkinson Williams.*

stream as far as the place known as Jacobs' Upper Salt Works. Here he tore his boat to pieces and built a shanty for his family to live in until he could build a house on his land. The first shanty made for his boys and John Case to live in while clearing the land was made of bark and sticks and stood near the ground afterwards used as a family graveyard.

Brewster Higley IV was a Revolutionary War soldier and served as justice of the peace in Vermont. General Arthur St. Clair, governor of the Northwest Territory, appointed Brewster Higley as one of the justices of the peace for the county of Washington. The commission bears the date December 28, 1801, and was done in Chillicothe. This commission, and one for Fuller Elliot of Letart, are probably the only commissions for justices appointed under the territorial government for the people living in what is now Meigs County. Mr. Higley was one of the first associate judges of Gallia County and served for a number of years. He was elected justice of the peace in Rutland Township and, in 1815, was made the second postmaster of Rutland. He died on June 20, 1847, at the old age of eighty-eight years, three months and six days. His wife, Naomi Higley, died on February 4, 1850, aged eighty-nine years, one month and three days.

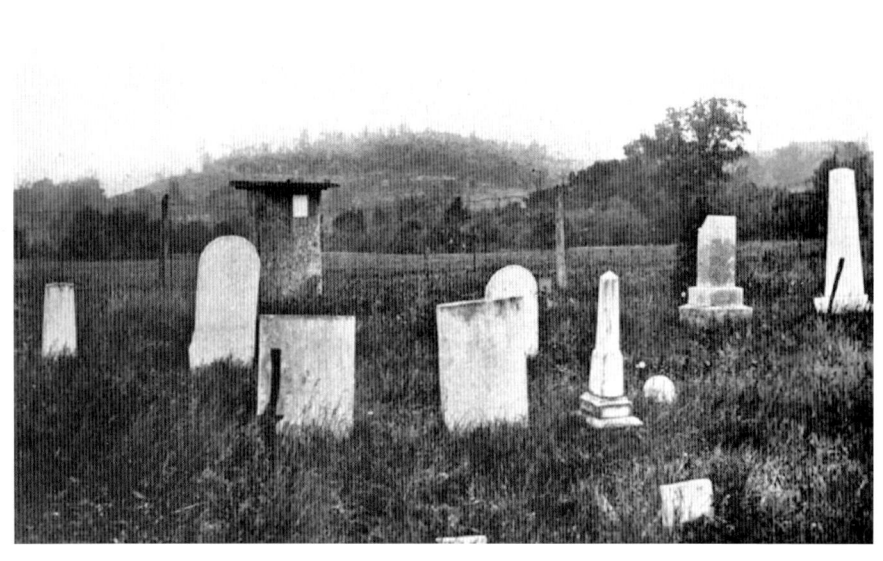

*Above*: Higley family graveyard. *From Kay Jenkinson Williams.*

*Left*: Dr. Brewster Higley VI. *From author's collection.*

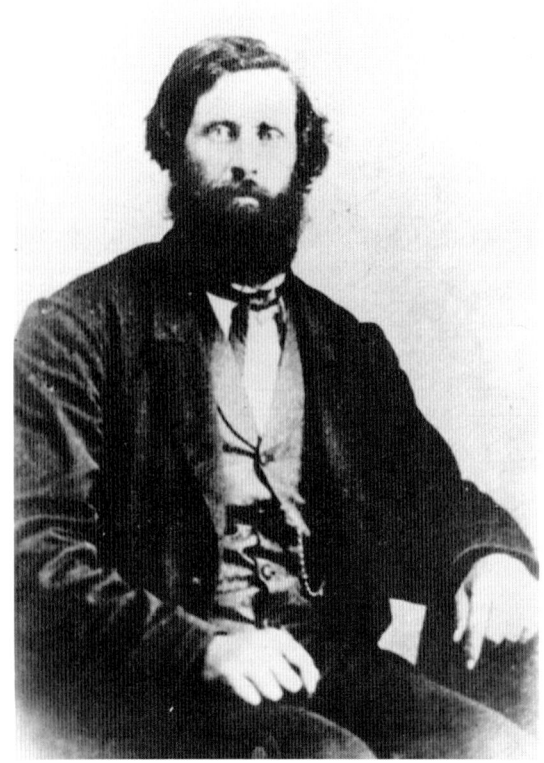

The most well-known Higley from Rutland, however, would be Dr. Brewster Higley VI, born in Rutland on November 30, 1823. Dr. Higley wrote the words that would become the unofficial anthem of the American West. In 1841, Higley VI began studying medicine at La Porte Medical College in La Porte, Indiana, at the age of eighteen. After graduating in 1849, he resettled in Pomeroy, Ohio, and established his first medical practice as an otolaryngologist—commonly known as an ear, nose and throat doctor.

He was married five times. His first three marriages are reported to have ended tragically, but there is some dispute whether this was the case with his second wife. Maria Winchell Higley, his first wife, died in 1852 from disease. Eleanor Page Higley was his second wife and mother of his son Brewster Higley VII. It was reported that Eleanor died soon after the birth of their son, but it was also reported that Eleanor may have taken their child and left Dr. Higley to live with her previous husband, David A. Smith. She likely died between 1853 and 1870. Catherine Livingston Higley was his third wife and mother of daughter Estella and son Arthur Herman. Catherine was injured in 1864 and subsequently died.

Mrs. Mercy Ann McPherson was his fourth wife, and Higley quite literally ran from this tumultuous marriage in 1871. The two had a wild relationship, and Dr. Higley felt compelled to leave his children with relatives in Illinois and secretly move away. He briefly practiced medicine in Indiana, then found his way to Smith County, Kansas, in 1871 to claim land under the Homestead Act of 1862. While he was there, his marriage to Mrs. McPherson dissolved by default on February 9, 1875. One month later, on March 8, he married Sarah Clemons, his final wife.

Dr. Higley was so inspired by his new rural surroundings that he decided to write a poem in praise of the Kansas prairie. In 1872, the lyrics to "Home on the Range" were originally published as a poem in the *Smith County Pioneer* under the title "My Western Home."

> Oh, give me a home where the buffalo roam,
> Where the deer and the antelope play;
> Where never is heard a discouraging word
> And the sky is not clouded all day.
>
> Oh, give me the gale of the Solomon vale
> Where life streams with buoyancy flow,
> On the banks of the Beaver, where seldom if ever
> Any poisonous herbage doth grow.

Oh, give me the land where the bright diamond sand
Throws light from the glittering stream;
Where glideth along the graceful white swan,
Like a maid in her heavenly dreams.

I love these wild flowers in this bright land of ours;
I love, too, the curlew's wild scream.
The bluffs of white rocks and antelope flocks
That graze on the hillsides so green.

How often at night, when the heavens are bright
By the light of the glittering stars,
Have I stood there amazed and asked as I gazed
If their beauty exceeds this of ours.

The air is so pure, the breezes so light,
The zephyrs so balmy at night,
I would not exchange my home here to range
Forever in azure so bright.

The music was later added by Daniel E. Kelley (1808–1905), a carpenter and friend of Higley's. Higley's original words are similar to those of the modern version of the song, but the original did not contain the words "on the range." The song was eventually adopted by ranchers, cowboys and other western settlers and spread across the United States in various forms. In 1925, the song was arranged as sheet music by Texas composer David W. Guion (1892–1981), who was occasionally credited as the composer. It was officially adopted as the state song of Kansas on June 30, 1947. In 2010, members of the Western Writers of America chose it as one of the top one hundred western songs of all time.

# Chapter 3

# LEVI STEDMAN

henever you look back at the early history of Meigs County, or more aptly, the area that would become Meigs County, you will see Levi Stedman's name appear in abundance. In Stillman Larkin Carter's 1908 *Pioneer History of Meigs County*, Stedman is mentioned thirty-four times, while Valentine B. Horton's name appears a mere twenty-one times. Levi Stedman is one of the forgotten pioneers of Meigs County.

Born on September 19, 1771, in Tunbridge, Orange County, Vermont, to Alexander Stedman (1746–1814) and Sarah Stedman, née Cushman (1748–1802), Levi Stedman was the second of nine children. He married Dorothy Cowdery on March 27, 1794, and the couple had ten children. Stedman and fellow traveler Peter Grow arrived in the territory that was to become Meigs County in 1798 and built their first cabins in the eventual town of Chester. A year later, their families joined them.

The Honorable Brewster Higley settled his family near the mouth of the middle fork of Leading Creek in the spring of 1799. At the same time, Stedman was building his gristmill. According to the *Pioneer History of Meigs County*,

> It became necessary that a road should be opened between [the mill and Mr. Higley's settlement]. Accordingly, it was agreed that Mr. Levi Stedman and a party from Shade [R]iver and a company from Leading [C]reek, under the direction of Mr. Brewster Higley, should meet near the place where little George Russell lived at the forks of Thomas

[C]reek. The parties…proceeded to mark out the road to their respective homes. The Leading [C]reek party marked the way very near where [it] is now established. When they passed through a very thick wood on what is now the Stow farm and on through the low gap to a place by the west line of the McGuire land…night had overtaken them, the darkness was intense, not a gleam of light to direct them, when one of their number thought of an expedient, which was to get into the channel of that little stream, exceedingly crooked as it was, and to follow its meanderings to the mouth, which was open ground, so they all got safely home. This occurred in 1804 or 1805.

Athens County was formed out of part of Washington County in 1805, and a year later Levi Stedman settled on more than 420 acres at the mouth of the Hockhocking River with his family. At this time, the Hockhocking served as the dividing line between Athens and Gallia Counties. Stedman lived on the Gallia County side about a half mile below the county line. In 1808, Stedman decided to annex all but one small section of his land to Athens County, creating the present Orange Township line. He went on to build the first log mill in Chester Township in 1808 on the Shade River. It survived until 1863 when it was destroyed during Confederate general John Hunt Morgan's infamous raid.

In 1811, Athens County removed part of Troy Township and created Rome Township. Stedman and other prominent early settlers Asahel Cooley and Daniel Stewart were part of the new township. Stedman moved within a year and returned to the area that would become the village of Chester. He opened a store, farmed, ran a sawmill, kept a tavern and owned a distillery. By 1812, Stedman was a justice of the peace and became the Chester area's first postmaster. In addition to Stedman's varied roles, Athens County records show him as a county commissioner in 1815, 1817 and 1818.

While delving into county politics, Stedman's businesses began changing hands. Dr. David Gardner and his brother Charles bought out the store and filled it with goods from New York, Boston and Philadelphia in 1818. Samuel Grant took charge of the logmill in 1820 and added new machinery.

Meigs County was formed from parts of Gallia and Athens Counties in 1819. In Edgar Ervin's *Pioneer History of Meigs County*, Ohio to 1949, he described how a farmhouse was used as the first county seat in Middleport, and the residents expected it to remain that way. Three commissioners were appointed to preside over county operations until October 1819, when successors would be elected. Levi Stedman, Elijah Runner and William

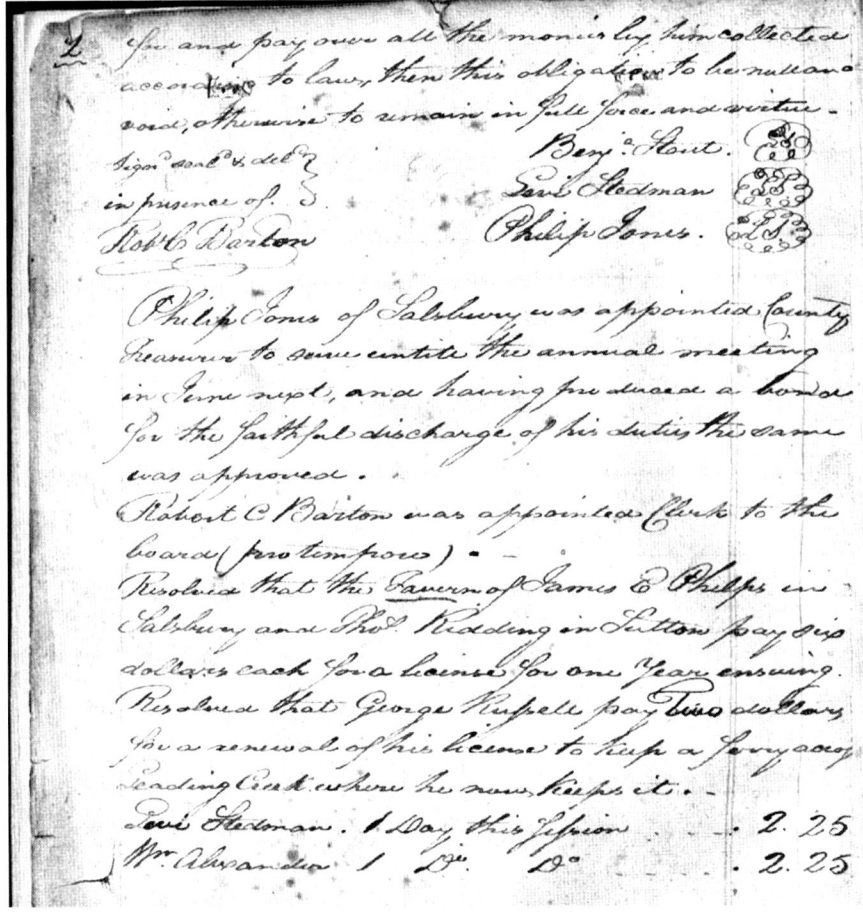

Signatures from the minutes of the first Meigs County commissioners' meeting. Note Levi Stedman's signature and seal. *From Gary Coleman.*

Alexander were appointed as Meigs County's first commissioners. After going through several seats of justice, ranging from "farmhouses to under a tree at some farmhouse," and a great struggle to fill county offices, the Ohio General Assembly appointed Elnathan Scofield of Fairfield County, Joseph Martin of Pike County and David Mitchell of Scioto County to find and create a fixed county seat.

Benjamin Smith offered twenty acres of land on the Ohio River in Middleport for the county seat. In April 1821, the general assembly adjourned without voting to grant the seat to be in Middleport. In April 1822, Meigs County commissioners John Barr, William Vance and William

Dunn selected fifty acres of land in Chester, and a courthouse was built that same year to be the permanent seat of Meigs County government. The land was donated by none other than Levi Stedman.

Stedman took ill and died at the age of fifty-one on January 29, 1823, and was buried at Chester Cemetery. Sometime in the early part of the nineteenth century, Levi Stedman became a master mason in Paramuthia Lodge No. 25 in Athens, Ohio. No record has been found of any of his Masonic rolls, though his tombstone bares the Square and Compasses.

# Chapter 4

# GREAT KIDNAPPING OF ADAM SMITH, 1824

T he year is 1824. John Quincy Adams, Andrew Jackson, William H. Crawford and Henry Clay are locked in a presidential election where no winner is declared, and it will go to the House of Representatives for the deciding vote. Adams is declared the winner. There are twenty-four stars on the U.S. flag and the Marquis de Lafayette arrives in the United States to tour all twenty-four of those states. Slavery is a top interest in national politics, and just like any other area, Meigs County takes interest in the issue. Most of Meigs County's citizens support the antislavery movement, including one of Meigs County's first settlers, Hamilton Kerr. The Underground Railroad has been running through Meigs County for about a year.

After slaves crossed the Ohio River, their first stop was at the home of Hamilton Kerr, near the mouth of Leading Creek. Kerr hired Adam Smith to act as a guide for fugitive slaves heading North, and he would follow the same route taken by slaves who had been freed by their masters. At this point, the former slaves would follow Leading Creek and Little Leading Creek through Rutland Township to the home of Horace Holt, a prominent manufacturer of weaving reed. From here, fugitive slaves would travel toward Albany. Despite being a well-traveled route, Smith would often run into trouble, either from lack of needed aid for the runaways or from their former owners, many of whom were from Virginia. West Virginia had not yet been made into a state, and slavery was legal in Virginia, which was on the southern border of the Ohio River at this time.

Slave owners on the Kanawha and Ohio Rivers upriver from Point Pleasant, Virginia (now West Virginia), sent detectives to both sides of the Ohio River to locate fugitive slaves. They came to the conclusion that Adam Smith was assisting fugitive slaves in their escape northward. In October 1824, four men from Virginia arrested Smith and forced him into the Point Pleasant Jail. The men took Smith by force and with no authority of law, all the while refusing to accept bail money for Smith's release. The people of Meigs County saw "this gross violation of the most sacred rights of the citizens of Ohio, showing such contempt for the state's jurisdiction, that it excited universal indignation and open violence was threatened to release Smith from his illegal confinement."

A vigilance committee was formed and set up lookout points ranging from Colonel Jones' Landing, where Mill Street in Middleport meets the Ohio River, and Smith's Landing, where the mouth of Silver Run meets the Ohio River. Additionally, there were lookouts from Silver Run to the home of John S. Giles in Rutland. These lookouts communicated from station to station through horns, and an alarm would circulate to every lookout within fifteen minutes if any suspicious person or group was seen.

Six weeks had passed since Adam Smith was arrested, and he was still being held in the Point Pleasant Jail. Around the same time, the Wagner family, a wealthy, slave-owning family, put one of their slaves in the jail with a plot to murder Smith. The slave was promised that if he killed Smith, the family would grant him freedom. Once Ohioans were made aware of this information, preparations to break Smith out of jail were put into effect. John S. Giles convinced Smith's guards to allow him to bring Smith clothing, and with that, Giles told Smith to be ready to escape at any moment.

In November, Giles and prominent Meigs County citizens Martin Meeker, William Hatch, John Woods, David Tyler, Obediah Ralph, William Terry and Charles Giles met at the mouth of Silver Run and, in blackface, headed downriver toward Point Pleasant in a pirogue (small boat). One man was armed with hunting rifles, pistols and a flintlock musket loaded with seven rifle bullets. Another man carried a dragoon, or horse pistol, loaded with three rifle bullets.

The men knew that the Point Pleasant Jail was heavily guarded but feared the imminent danger to Smith's life. The crew floated with muffled oars and landed eleven miles downriver from Silver Run at Point Pleasant. Martin Meeker and Charles Giles each took a musket and confined four guards to a room in the upstairs of the jail. Downstairs one of the party took an ax to the prison door, busted it down, ran inside the cell, grabbed Smith—half asleep in his bunk—and attempted to make their escape. The party began to make a retreat back to the river with Smith, but the guards came out onto a platform on the second story of the jail and prepared to fire.

Rescuer John Woods fired his dragoon pistol, but it misfired. The audacity of Woods's action kept the guards from immediately firing on the rescue party. The party was getting into the boat when a jailer and a guard who followed the party began firing on them. William Terry returned fire on the guards and hit one in the ear, causing him to fall to the ground. As the boat made it to the middle of the river, additional guards appeared and fired on the rescue party. The pirogue was bombarded with musket balls, requiring them to turn broadside to the shore while all the men, except David Tyler, lay in the boat in an attempt to shield themselves. As a result, Tyler was shot in the chest but survived with a five-inch scar.

The boat eventually made it downstream and out of range of all the guns except that of one jailer who followed them and took up a position behind a sycamore tree on the edge of the riverbank. His shots were "an annoyance to the rescue party." John S. Giles gave the order for the men in the rescue party to begin firing at the jailer. One of the shots hit the tree and caused wood splinters to burst from it, which severely injured the jailer's eyes. The rescue party then had to abandon the boat and walk home, making sure to be quiet and avoid disturbing their spouses, who were unaware of the events that their husbands had planned and carried out.

The Virginians in Point Pleasant were furious about the events that occurred and talked of going to Meigs County to capture John S. Giles, John Woods and Elisha Ayres to take them to Point Pleasant to be lynched. However, they opted to take a more lawful approach and had indictment charges brought against Smith's rescuers. James Pleasants, governor of Virginia, made a requisition to Jeremiah Morrow, governor of Ohio, to surrender the three to Virginia authorities. Morrow agreed and deputized Colonel Lewis of Virginia to make the arrest. When Colonel Lewis crossed the river into Meigs County, citizens were unaware of his authority and prepared to make a defense. Colonel Lewis went directly to the county seat in Chester and called on Thomas Rairdon of Long Bottom, Constable Dickey of Chester Township and a deputy sheriff with a last name of Newsom. The four men went to the home of John S. Giles to make the arrest. Giles, Woods and Ayres went without resistance.

Halfway between Giles's home and Point Pleasant, a party of twelve men in disguise came out of the woods on Sargent's Hill demanding Giles's release. Giles convinced the men of Colonel Lewis's authority from the governor of Ohio and of his willingness to let the law take its course.

Giles, Woods and Ayres were placed in the Point Pleasant jail for two months before they were tried. Giles and Ayres were both found not guilty, but Woods was found guilty and fined thirty dollars. Woods refused to pay and refused to allow his friends to pay his fine and decided to serve time in the jail, refusing to leave until they kicked him out.

# Chapter 5

# JOSHUA GARDNER AND THE SLAVE CASE IN THE OHIO SUPREME COURT

T he Mason-Dixon line was surveyed between 1763 and 1767 by Charles Mason and Jeremiah Dixon in the resolution of a border dispute involving Maryland, Pennsylvania and Delaware. Later— but before the Missouri Compromise—it became known as the border between the northern United States and the southern United States. The Ohio River is sometimes considered the western extension of the Mason-Dixon line. Due its narrowness, the Ohio was the way to freedom for thousands of slaves escaping to the North, and many whites and free blacks helped the Underground Railroad resistance movement. In Meigs County, the Underground Railroad was in operation for around forty years prior to the start of the Civil War. Many of Meigs County's early pioneers came from the New England area and were hard-nosed abolitionists who hated slavery with a passion. It didn't take long for these pioneers to help runaway slaves on their journeys northward.

Caleb Gardiner was born on November 1, 1763. He married Phoebe Gorton on March 30, 1786, and then married Lydia Thurston on November 1, 1789, both in Connecticut. His son, Joshua Gardner, was born on January 5, 1793, in Stonington, New London, Connecticut. Sometime after 1793, he moved to New York for a while and finally moved to Rutland in 1803. On April 29, 1819, twenty-eight days after Meigs County was founded, Gardiner married Nancy Ann Caldwell. According to Meigs County's section of the *Harris History*, "Many of the early settlers were of Puritan stock, and thoroughly imbued with the love of liberty, united to dauntless courage and daring to aid or rescue from oppression any helpless fellow being. Aiding escaping slaves came naturally to these people."

The Wagner family had been one of the earliest to settle in what is now Mason County, West Virginia, formerly Virginia. The Wagners owned most of the land opposite Pomeroy and kept more than one hundred slaves. You could imagine the aggravation the Wagners felt when their slaves would escape across the river to Meigs County, especially after the growing hostility brought on by the kidnapping of Adam Smith in 1824, which fueled even more animosity on opposite sides of the Ohio River.

Joshua Gardner's story as an Underground Railroader is certainly an interesting one, and it cost him everything he had. His son, Albert C. Gardner, repeated the following story as told to him by his father.

One morning in the early part of summer in 1825, a group of neighbors were at the blacksmith shop of Joseph Giles, near New Lima. Among this group was Joshua Gardner, who lived nearby. A horseman was seen approaching from the direction of Scipio, and as he came fully into view, it could be seen that a slave woman sat on the horse with the stranger. It was evident that she was not a willing passenger, so the horseman was promptly halted. Mr. Gardner demanded to know of the man's authority in taking the woman.

He had none. The man said that "she acknowledged herself to be a slave of the Wagners' in Virginia," opposite Kerr's Run in Ohio. She had made her escape from bondage and was on her way to Canada to join her husband, who had made the race for freedom sometime before. Mr. Gardner told them that he was a peace officer—a town constable—and it was his duty to prevent kidnapping, as well as other crimes. Turning to the woman, he asked her "if she wanted to go with this man."

She sobbed out, "No, sir."

Mr. Gardner told her to "get down and go where you please," and as an officer of the law, he would protect her. She slipped down from the horse and started to retrace the road from which she came.

The man started for Virginia to inform the Wagners and send them on her track. Some of the party from the shop soon overtook the woman and guided her to the house of a Mr. Crandle, a poor, but noble, citizen who lived in an "out-of-the-way" place, where she could be provided for until the search and excitement died away. The colored woman was hidden in an old brush fence by a shelving rock. Mrs. Crandle and the family fed and took care of her. The Wagners were soon in the neighborhood, scouring the country and offering rewards.

On one occasion, a very poor man from the east side of the township was loitering around the Crandle's premises in search of deer or turkey and discovered the hiding place of the woman. Tempted by the reward, he started to inform the slave owners but first stopped at Stephen Ralph's and told him of his plan and visions of future wealth. As soon as he left, Ralph shouldered his rifle and, marching through the woods, gave the alarm.

By the next morning, a fire had destroyed the old brush fence and destroyed all traces of its recent occupant. The Wagners concluded that the old hunter was a willful fraud. The woman was removed to the farm of Benjamin Bellows and secreted away until he had communicated with parties in Canada and ascertained the whereabouts of the woman's husband. Mr. Bellows prepared a wagon with a false bottom, or double box. He put the woman in the bottom box, and on the top, he put a lot of Weaver's reeds and started out for Canada to sell them. Mr. Bellows reported that he traveled one day with one of the Wagners and another party who were hunting this very woman, and Mr. Wagner got off from his horse and helped Bellows's wagon down a steep, rocky hill to keep it from turning over, little suspecting that the object of his search was so near him.

Foiled in all other points, the Wagners determined to try the law to obtain the value of their woman chattel from Joshua Gardner. Suit was brought in the Court of Common Pleas at Chester and came to trial by jury, which resulted in a verdict for the plaintiffs. An appeal was taken, and the Supreme Court held that the admissions and sayings of the woman could not be admitted to prove her identity; if she was a competent witness, she must be produced in court, but if she was a slave, she could not be a competent witness. So, the case failed.

According to Marcus Bosworth, after the trial, Supreme Court judge Pease was heard to say, "An action of trover for the recovery of stock might do in Virginia, but it would not do in Ohio unless the stock had more than two legs."

The next step was to kidnap Gardner and deal with him according to the rules of chivalry. It was reported that twelve men were seen on horseback in disguise for that purpose, but they were anticipated by a force abundantly able to resist them. There was no attack made. The expenses of this suit and trouble consequently consumed all of Mr. Gardner's property. In 1849, he made an overland trip with the party called the Buckeye Rovers to California to recoup his fortune. He did and returned with enough gold dust to buy a comfortable home in Rutland, Ohio, where he enjoyed the respect and confidence of his neighbors until he was seventy-seven years old. He died on March 1, 1869, in Rutland.

## Chapter 6

# EARLY PIONEER HUNTING STORIES

An account of hunting adventures in 1832, as described by Mr. John Warth and reported by his relative Mr. Silas Jones in 1832, shows that Mr. Warth never tired of entertaining his guests with narratives of peril and adventure in his early life. Mr. Jones reported—as near as possible—in the actor's own words:

In the time of great peril, when it was not safe to look out of the fort, and our brother Robert had been shot while chopping a log near the fort, it became necessary to procure some meat for the families in the fort. Thinking the Ohio bottoms less liable to be infested with Indians, George and I stole out of the fort at night, and paddled noiselessly down the river to a point opposite Blennerhasset Island, where we hid our canoe in the willows. As soon as it was light we started in different directions to hunt for deer. I had not gone half a mile when I saw two tall savages coming in the direction I was going. I squatted in the high pea vines and thick undergrowth that covered the ground while they passed by near me but did not see me. However, they soon discovered my trail, which they followed back to the canoe, which I supposed they would watch until the owner would come.

My great concern now was the safety of my brother George, as he not being aware [sic] of the presence of the Indians would return to the canoe and fall prey to them. Then I decided on a plan to save George, which was to proceed to a point out of sight of the Indians, hide my gun, swim across the river, then swim to the island and watch for

George's return. This plan I fully carried out. Along in the afternoon I heard the report of my brother's gun after which my anxiety amounted to agony—minutes seemed hours. At length I saw George coming out of the woods with the carcass of a deer on his back. He looked up and down the shore, when I got his attention and by signs and gestures got him to take in the situation. We both regained the fort without further trouble. When the danger was over I went with a party and recovered my gun and the canoe.

Another anecdote from Mr. Warth:

Another time George and I went out in search of game, and were separated some distance, when I heard the report of his gun, after which I heard cries of distress coming from George. I ran to him with all the possible speed of my limbs, and found him pinned to the earth by a large elk. I was so exhausted that I could not draw the bead, so I ran up and thrust the muzzle of my rifle against the animal's ribs and fired, when he fell dead at my feet. My brother was not much hurt, the horns of the elk had not penetrated through the ample folds of his hunting shirt, which held him to the ground. The hunter's shirt was made sufficiently large so that he could stow a week's provisions above the belt.

George had fired on the elk, only wounding him, and so enraging the beast that he turned on the hunter and compelled George to take refuge in a high upturned root where he fought with his clubbed rifle till he had nothing left but the bent barrel, when the maddened elk finally dislodged him, with the above result. Our capture was a valuable one, but did not compensate for George's gun.

# AN ENCOUNTER WITH WOLVES AT SHADE RIVER

George Warth and Peter Niswonger took their rifles and went out for a hunt. After traveling some time, they came to a ridge that ran near the mouth of Shade River. Warth said to Niswonger, "You go on the bottom on one side of the ridge and I will take the other side and will come together at the end of the ridge on the bank of Shade River." They started thus, but Niswonger got out of the way and came out above the second ridge.

Warth went directly to the river end of the ridge, and there sat seven to ten wolves. They showed no alarm at his approach—the largest walked toward him, and the others followed. He shot the foremost one, and it fell dead. He reloaded his rifle as soon as he could because the wolves indicated they would fight. Then he went into the river until the water was up to his hips, and the wolves went in after him. He shot the foremost one through the shoulder, and he went back to the water's edge and sat down and looked at Warth. He defended himself with his empty rifle by breaking the stock in many pieces and fighting them with the empty barrel.

He had the advantage of being deep enough to outswim the wolves, and he pounded them until they retreated to the edge of the water and sat down on their haunches and looked at him. He dared not get out of the water, as he might not be able to fight if they followed him. Soon Niswonger came to the shore opposite the wolves and Warth crossed over to him and told him "not to shoot—we will call it a draw game, neither party whipped." He would not let Niswonger shoot, as they could be attacked. The hunters returned to their homes on Old Town Creek, and the next day, they increased their force and went back to the place of the battle and found two dead wolves but no live ones.

Warth wasn't the only one going on hunting adventures at this time. Black bears were numerous in these parts of southern Ohio in the first years of the nineteenth century. Henry Roush of Letart Township related an incident of his encounter with bears:

> I was going out to bring in the cows, and contrary to my usual custom did not take my rifle with me, and while passing along the rear of my neighbor's field of corn I saw two young bears helping themselves to roasting ears. I succeeded in capturing one of them, which began to squall at a furious rate, which brought the mother bear rushing upon me with great fury. I had to drop my prize and run for a high fence which was near, with the angry bear at my heels. After gaining the top of the fence, I seized a stake and beat off my assailants.

Elk were seen but not in great numbers. Wolves were numerous and very troublesome. It was as common to hear the howl of a wolf in the twilight of an evening as it was to hear the crowing of a rooster in the morning. They would answer each other from hill to hill when gathering their packs to prey on the settlers' sheep or young cattle.

In 1827, parties of people from the area were cutting out a road from Chester, the county seat of Meigs County, to Sterling Bottom, on the Ohio River. At a certain point they lay out a road from here to Old Town. The overseers of the road construction were Nehemiah Bicknell and Samuel Bowman, as well as one or two other men. They had progressed only halfway from Chester when night came on, and they had to spend the night in the woods. They built fires for protection from wolves, whose howling they heard all night at no great distance. The men kept the fires burning but slept little.

Wolves with dens somewhere around the head of Ground Hog Creek and Old Town Creek continued to prey on the farmers' sheep in Lebanon Township. An expert trapper named Allen came from Washington County in 1840 and successfully exterminated these wolves.

The panther was often met by the hunter but was easily killed, as the animal was of a bold, defiant nature and would climb a tree where he was an easy mark for the hunter's rifle. Deer were found in great numbers and were a great blessing to the pioneer families who depended on the wild game for meat. Venison was a choice meat, and the deer hides were tanned to make various articles of apparel. Gray foxes were numerous and were great enemies to poultry, but the red fox seemed to supersede the gray, and neither were seen in later years. The raccoon was a great pest, destroying large quantities of corn while still green and on the stalk. Racoon hunting with dogs was a common sport for boys until the animal disappeared. The opossum and red and gray squirrel remain in limited numbers.

*Chapter 7*

# CHOLERA EPIDEMICS

*Those who cannot remember the past are condemned to repeat it.*
—*George Santayana*

*H*ow will they repeat it, you may ask? An example today is the hepatitis epidemic happening at fast-food restaurants all around our region. What causes this disease to be transmitted? According to an article in an April 2018 edition of the *Dayton Daily News*, "Hepatitis A is a vaccine-preventable, communicable disease of the liver caused by the hepatitis A virus….It is usually transmitted person-to-person through contact with an infected person's stool, or consumption of contaminated food or water." In other words, unsanitary health practices.

Looking back at the first half of the nineteenth century, the world had a different epidemic from unsanitary health practices: cholera. According to *Webster's Dictionary*, cholera is "an infectious and often fatal bacterial disease of the small intestine, typically contracted from infected water supplies and causing severe vomiting and diarrhea." It is usually spread by unsafe water and food contaminated with human feces that contain the bacteria. This was not our first bout with infectious diseases. Meigs County fell subject to not one but two epidemics over a fifteen-year span—first in 1834 and again in 1849.

Cholera first appeared in the United States in 1832—most likely from European immigrants, as the first cases reported were in New York and New Orleans, where many were arriving. In Ohio, Cleveland reported the first

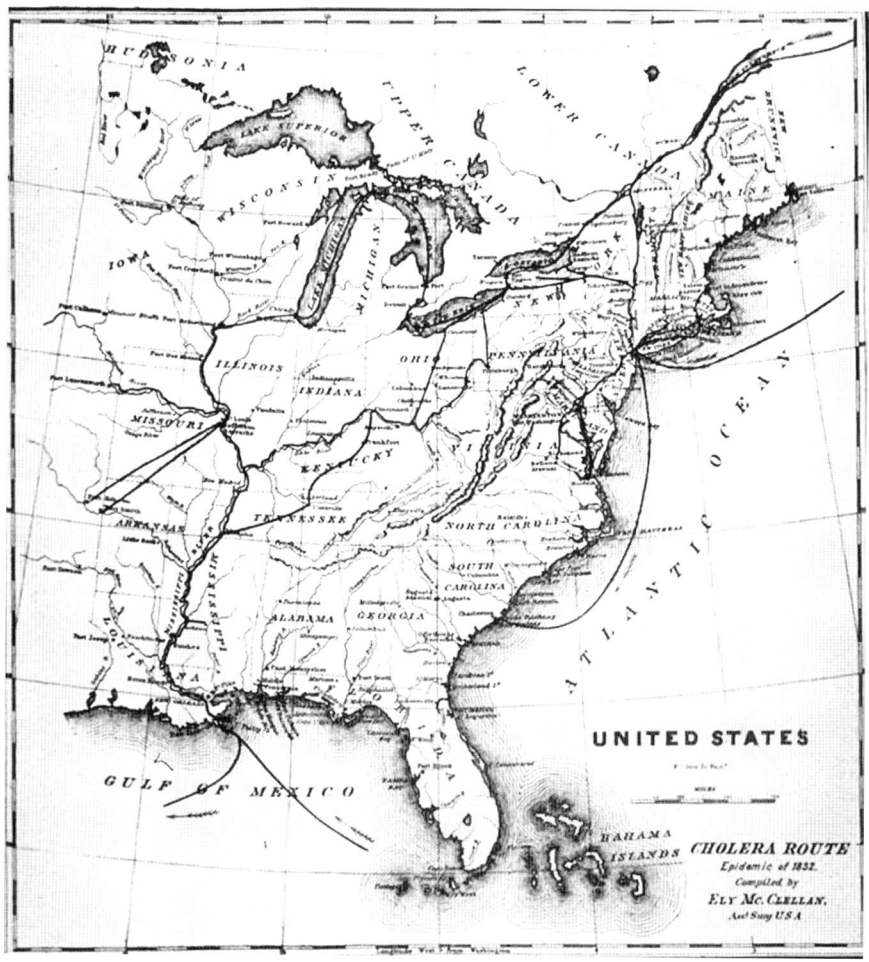

Route of the cholera epidemic of 1832. *From author's collection.*

death from the disease. That same year, the first recorded Meigs County citizen died of the disease. Barzillai Hosmer Miles, a minister from Rutland, died while returning from Louisiana to Meigs County. While the location of Barzillai's grave is not known, it is ironic that his family owned the land that would eventually become Miles Cemetery, where Barzillai's father, John Miles, was buried years later.

The year before the first major cholera outbreak in Meigs County, a steamboat approached a household in Lebanon Township, seeking permission to bury a man from the boat in the small graveyard nearby. The request was denied due to the homeowner's fear of cholera, and the man was interred along the roadside instead.

The first of countless reported cases of cholera in Meigs County occurred in July 1834. Dr. James S. Hibbard was called from Chester to Syracuse to tend to a man who had returned from a steamboat trip and was sick with severe vomiting and diarrhea. Larkin's *Pioneer History of Meigs County* states:

> Dr. Hibbard pronounced the case cholera and prescribed accordingly. On his way back to Chester he was attacked with the malady and, getting off from his horse, took a dose of calomel, lay down by the roadside and fell asleep in the woods. As soon as he was able to remount his horse he proceeded homeward. He finally recovered.

That same year, six-year-old Marcus Bosworth Jr. "went to bed as usual, but later called his mother, 'so very sick,' and, although medicine was administered at once, by 10 o'clock the child was dead." The epidemic was so severe that Van Weldon, a local cabinetmaker, had to switch from making cabinets to making coffins. Downriver in Cincinnati, coal delivered from Pomeroy was burned on every street corner in hopes that it could stop the disease from spreading.

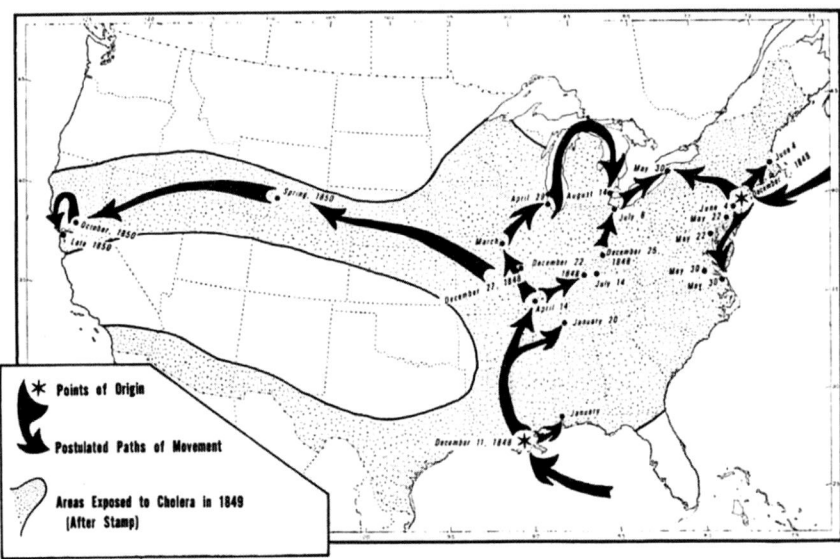

Route of the cholera epidemic of 1849. *From author's collection.*

## Cholera.

The Board of Health report the following deaths by cholera since last report: Mrs. Weldon; Frances Cohen; Mrs. Hanke; Rev. Mr. Schwartz; Mrs. Findling; Mrs. Neubauer; C. Herp.

Most of these deaths have occurred since Saturday. Four or five other cases of cholera have been reported to the Board. Most of these, however, are recovering. I. KNAPP,
Sec'y Board of Health.

Local cholera deaths announced in *Meigs County Telegraph*, August 31, 1852. *From author's collection.*

During the second epidemic, in 1849, several cholera deaths were noted in Pomeroy and Letart; however, the first reported deaths from cholera in that year were members of the Bailey family from Middleport. Cholera claimed the lives of David Bailey, his wife, daughter, son-in-law and sister, Mrs. Hudson. According to *The Autobiography of Dr. Thomas H. Barton: The Self-Made Physician of Syracuse, Ohio,*

> The smoke of tobacco was regarded as a preventative and many persons, even women and small boys, had cigars almost constantly in their mouths. Others placed full confidence in garlic…some chewed it constantly, others kept it in their pockets and shoes. Even the time-honored custom of hand shaking fell into disrepute and many recoiled with affright at even the [offer] of a hand.

In Columbus, 116 inmates at the Ohio penitentiary succumbed to the illness. In 1849, former president James Polk, a resident of Tennessee, was the most famous person to die of cholera. Cholera resulted in the postponement of the first Ohio State Fair and the Ohio Constitutional Convention of

1850–51. Eight thousand people died in Cincinnati during this epidemic, including Harriet Beecher Stowe's infant son.

Unfortunately for people stricken with cholera, the treatment was almost as bad as the illness. Doctors routinely prescribed calomel, which contained mercury, and numerous people died from mercury poisoning or suffered other ill effects from this drug. As sanitation improved within the United States, including chlorination of water, the illness became less common. Today, the standard treatment for cholera is to keep the ill person hydrated with germ-free water or other fluids—none of which include mercury.

*Chapter 8*

# THE CROSS FAMILY'S BUSINESSES

*It is easier to do a job right than to explain why you didn't.*
*—President Martin Van Buren*

These words could sum up the legacy the Cross family's businesses gave the people of Sutton Township, and all of Meigs County, into the twenty-first century, when Cross' Son's Grocery went out of business. At that time, not only did the longest-operating business in Meigs County close, but so did one of the oldest businesses in the Northwest Territory.

Lucius Cross was born on December 30, 1798, in Mansfield, Connecticut. By the time he was three years old, Lucius had been orphaned and brought to Marietta, Ohio, where he grew up on a farm. It is said that Lucius's stepmother stole his inheritance and used it to educate her own son, John Brough, who became the twenty-sixth governor of Ohio from January 11, 1864, to August 29, 1865.

In April 1822, Lucius married Thirza Stanley, daughter of Washington County's Timothy Stanley, and the couple went directly to Meigs County, settling on lands behind Graham's Station in what is now Racine. In 1823, Lucius built a log cabin to live in, prepared his land for cultivation and built a tannery on his farm.

Lucius Cross went on to operate a trade of boats loaded with pressed hay and farm products in the South, and due to his many different industries and diverse interests, he gave employment to many men. In 1832, he built his large, spacious farmhouse. According to Larkin's *Pioneer History of Meigs County*, Mr. Cross was said to be "a real temperance man, and suffered no whisky to be brought to his premises, and his farm house has the record of being the first building erected in Meigs County without whisky or any intoxicating drink." The house, considered the best in Meigs County, was noted for its beauty in construction and location.

In 1836, Lucius erected a saw- and gristmill on Bowman's Run and founded the Racine Woolen Mill to build flatboats on the river at Graham's Station. Lucius used all of his timber for lumber, cordwood or tanbark. The mill was built from lumber cut and sawed at Lucius's water-powered sawmill on the farm. The mill was a three-story, twenty-eight-by-forty-foot structure that included a basement. The millstones, each weighing one ton, were made underground in France and then shipped overseas to Cross.

Two dams along the site allowed water to be shuttled to the waterwheel to power the mill. Thanks to an undependable water supply, though, the mill was changed to be powered by steam in 1915. During this time, the mill produced flour, bran, animal feed and cornmeal. The mill closed in 1917 due to lack of demand, and it sat vacant until Theodore Ebersbach purchased it, had it dismantled from its Bowman's Run location and rebuilt it behind the Meigs County Farm Bureau building (also known as MGM and Landmark) in Pomeroy. Today the mill welcomes visitors into Star Mill Park in Racine, where it was reassembled after the demolition of the Farm Bureau property in Pomeroy. All that remains of the Bowman's Run location is a chimney, foundation rocks and two of the original millstones.

In 1840, Lucius and Thirza built and established a trading post on their Bowman's Run farm to provide accommodation to their employees. In 1860, they built a store in Racine, which opened shortly before the first shells fired on Fort Sumter, heralding the beginning of the Civil War in 1861. It was in Racine that Lucius's son Waid began his career as a merchant. Lucius also had some military knowledge and drilled recruits for the Union army.

Lucius was entirely blind a few years before his death in August 1883. At his death, he left a valuable estate, a widow and nine sons and daughters. The sons were enterprising men, and most members of the family married and settled in Racine and the surrounding area. The exception was Edwin Cross who became a physician and took his profession to Chicago with notable success.

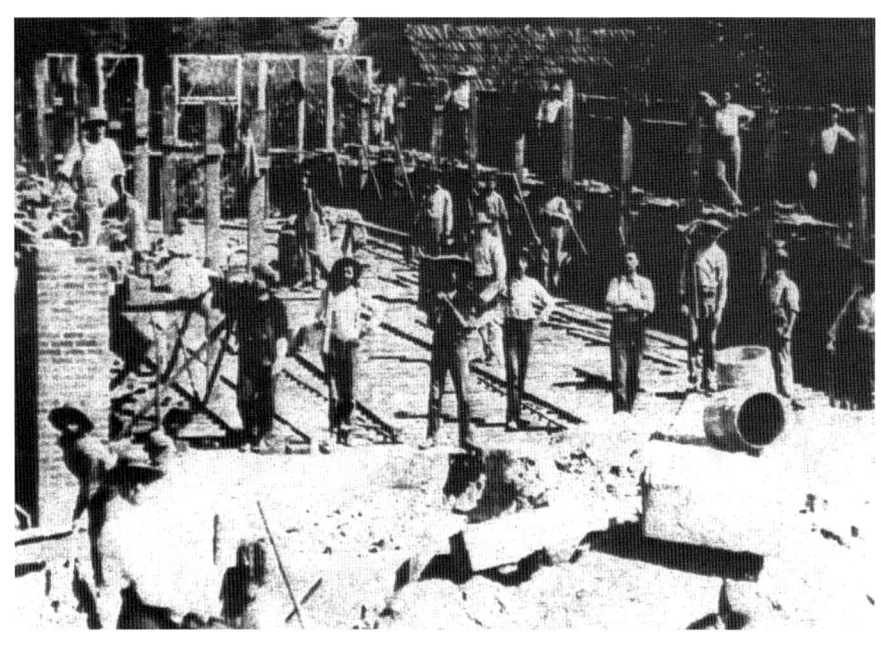

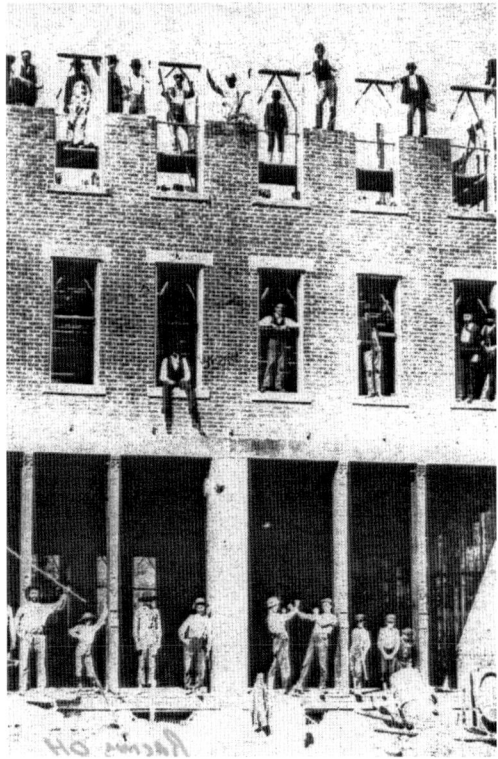

Building the larger Cross' Store in Racine in 1892. *From Pam Cross Wise.*

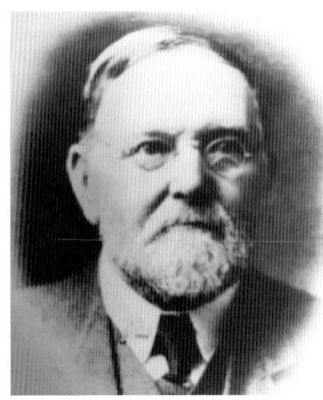

Waid Cross. *From Pam Cross Wise.*

Lucius's son Waid married Adeline Electa Miles in 1859, and they had five sons and two daughters: Harvey W. Cross, who died at only eight months (1860–1861); Mary Edani Cross, who died at age nine (1862–1872); Stanley Miles Cross (1865–1941); Charles Welles Cross (1867–1911); Electa May Cross Roberts (1870–1928); Benjamin Eber Cross (1873–1930); and John Waid Cross (1875–1955.)

In 1892, to meet rising demands, Waid decided to build a larger store across the street from the original two-story building in Racine. This unoccupied structure still stands today at 414 Pearl Street. The following twenty years proved to be flourishing times for Waid. With the new building came an additional business venture and partnership. Charles, Waid's third son, and Waid's son-in-law Dale R. Roberts established a hardware store in the former Cross' Store that sat across the street from the new grocery store.

Waid went on to start the Racine Banking Company, which became the First National Bank of Racine. After merging with the Racine Home Bank, the enterprise became Home National Bank of Racine. It is said that ever since Waid founded the Racine Banking Company, he has had a direct descendant employed by the organization.

According to the *Harris History*,

> Before Waid died on February 18, 1912, his daughter, Electa May Roberts and son-in-law Dale entered into a conspiracy on or about May 10, 1911, for the purpose of uttering and publishing certain deeds to several tracts of land belonging to Waid Cross. The resulting trial was very expensive and left very little room for continued growth.

After Waid's death, sons Stanley and John became owners of the store. This partnership continued until Stanley's death on November 5, 1941. Stanley's 50 percent interest in the business was willed to his two sons, John Dillon "Dee" Cross and Miles S. Cross, putting the business into a three-way partnership. John decided to retire in the early 1950s, and the store became sole property of Dee and Miles. Miles died on June 10, 1956,

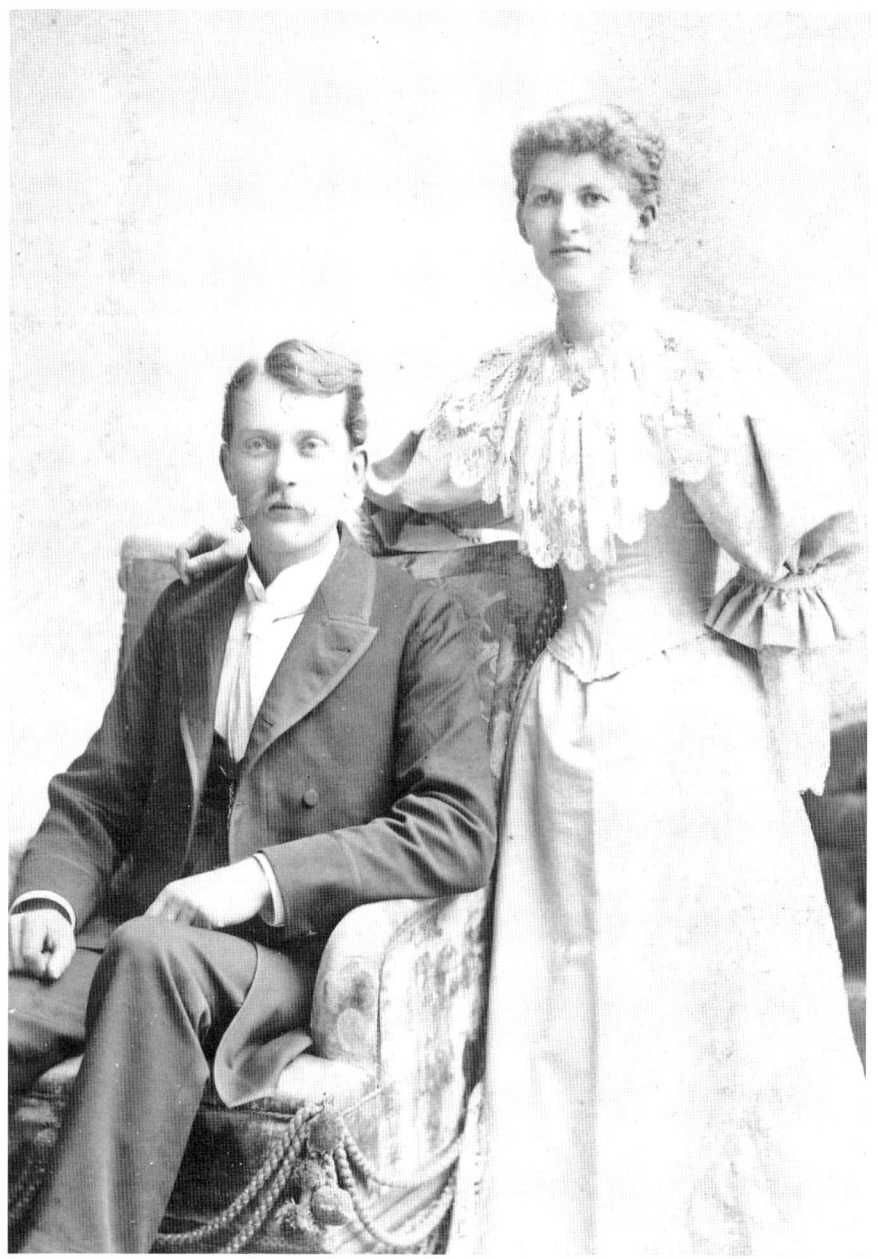

Stanley Miles Cross and his wife, Hattie M. Richards Cross. Stanley and his brother John took over operations of Cross' Store. *From author's collection.*

and his wife, Elsie, inherited his half of the business. Two years later, Dee purchased Elsie's half of the store to become the sole owner, then brought in his son William S. "Bill" Cross to help operate the business. In 1968, Bill became the only owner and operated the business until it closed in June 2000. Bill is the great-great-grandson of Lucius and the last son in direct succession to own the store.

# Chapter 9

# NELSON STORY

Nelson Story was born to Ira and Hannah Story on April 4, 1838, in Burlingham, Ohio. Ira and Hannah were originally from New Hampshire, and Nelson was their youngest son. By the time he turned eighteen, both of his parents had died. After trying his hand at teaching school and then spending two years at Ohio University, Story headed west to Kansas Territory. He made his way to the army post of Fort Leavenworth, where he was hired as a bullwhacker, or teamster (someone who would drive pack animals across long distances). By 1862, Story was hauling goods out of Denver, Colorado, and on one trip to Missouri he met Ellen Trent. They were married later that year in Kansas. By 1863, Story, tired of the teamster life, decided to try his hand as a prospector in the Montana gold fields.

By June, Story had mined about $30,000 worth of gold around Alder Gulch, Montana. By today's standards, Nelson Story would have amassed nearly $607,000 worth of gold. During his tenure in Montana, Story went on to become a charter member of one of Montana's first Masonic Lodges and served on a vigilance committee—a group voluntarily enforcing law and order. Story decided to trade his $30,000 worth of gold for $20,000 cash.

Story traveled to Fort Worth, Texas, and purchased one thousand cattle (although some sources say it was closer to three thousand) for around ten dollars a head. At this time, cattle could be purchased for very little in Texas due to post-Confederate economies and high supply because of eastern and British interest in the market. From April to December 1866, Story battled jayhawkers in Kansas after being denied the ability to load cattle on trains due to fear of disease. He then decided to take cattle up the Bozeman Trail. During that drive, Story defied orders from Colonel Henry B. Carrington of the United States Army to stop his advance north because of the threat of Indians. Story eventually fought Sioux and Crow Indians in Wyoming while on his way to Montana. Fortunately for Story's crew of around thirty, only one died and two were injured in the drive from Texas to Montana. While there were not the first cattle to be driven to Montana, it was the first herd to be driven from Texas to Montana.

Once he arrived in Bozeman, Montana, Story sold some of his cattle to miners at an astounding profit, making ten times more than he paid for them in Texas. The other cattle were kept, and Story started his own ranch in Paradise Valley, Montana. In 1882, Story opened the Story Flour Mill at the mouth of Bridger Creek, producing up to one hundred bushels of flour a day. Story was the major supplier of beef and flour for the U.S. Army at Fort Ellis and Fort C.F. Smith, as well as for the nearby Indian reservations in southeastern Montana. This business deal eventually made Story the first millionaire in Bozeman.

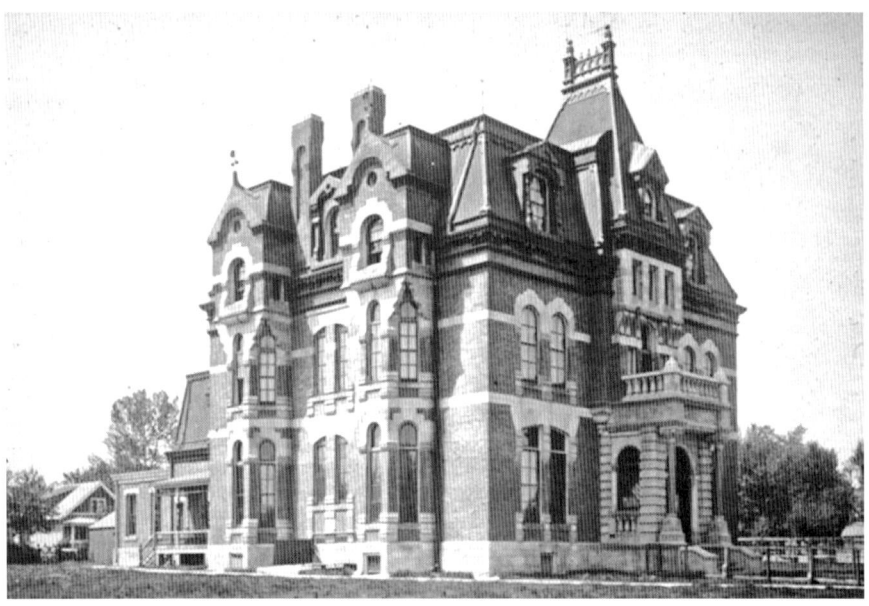

Nelson Story's ornate mansion in Bozeman, Montana. *From author's collection.*

In 1876, the army accused him of defrauding the Crow Nation by filling pork barrels with offal (animal entrails), double-counting single sacks of flour, passing off calves as full-grown cattle and attempting to bribe an officer. Story never stood trial, reportedly later boasting about avoiding prosecution by bribing the grand jurors. He also possessed a terrible temper, which resulted in violence on more than one occasion. According to one account, Story was notorious for pistol- or cane-whipping those who incurred his wrath and once threw a brick at his own son in anger.

With his fortune, Story eventually built a mansion on West Main Street in Bozeman. It was so elaborate and grand in design that it was often mistaken as the Gallatin County Courthouse, which sat across the street.

According to the *Bozeman Daily Chronicle*,

> Story and his wife Ellen had a son, Walter Perry Story, who was born in Bozeman, Montana, on December 18, 1882. He was the last born of their children. Walter began his education but later attended Shattuck Military Academy at Faribault, Minnesota. He left there in 1902 and graduated from Eastman Business College at Poughkeepsie, New York in 1903. He returned to Bozeman to work with his father until 1905, when he went to Los Angeles. There he worked in real estate and founded the first motor transit line in the western United States. He then helped his father develop more business in Los Angeles, including building the Story Building, which had twelve stories and was completed on April 1, 1910. The elder Story then retired and moved back to Bozeman but died in Los Angeles on March 10, 1926. Walter began his military service by enlisting as a private, later serving in World War I. He was out of the military until 1920 when he was commissioned as a captain of infantry in the California National Guard. He became a Brigadier General in July 1926. He wasn't promoted to Major General for another 11 years. In 1928 he founded Camp Merriam, which is now known as Camp San Luis Obispo. He entered federal military service in March 1941 and took command of the 40th Infantry Division. He was relieved of command in September 1941, and retired from active list in July 1942.

Nelson Story died at the age of eighty-seven and is buried at Sunset Hills Cemetery in Bozeman, Montana. In 1959, he was inducted into the National Cowboy Hall of Fame in Oklahoma City, Oklahoma, as a Great Westerner. In 2008, he was inducted into the Montana Cowboy Hall of Fame as a founding legacy member.

# Chapter 10

# CARMI ALDERMAN

uthor Barbara Lieberman said, "One does not seek love….It should find you all on its own." That is most certainly the case for Carmi Alderman, who found his way from Morgan County to life and love in Letart Falls.

Carmi Alderman was born on April 21, 1826, in Morgan County, Ohio. His parents, Hosea and Hannah, were both Puritans. They moved to Morgan County from Central New York with several members of their extended families and settled in various places. The name Carmi is of biblical origin. In Genesis 46:9, it is noted that Carmi is the last named of the four sons of Ruben, and notably, Carmi Alderman was the fourth son of eight children born to Hosea and Hannah.

It's noted in Edgar Ervin's *Pioneer History of Meigs County* that Carmi was an avid reader and had planned on obtaining a college education. Unfortunately, on October 21, 1843, when Carmi was seventeen, Hosea passed away. As if that weren't tragic enough, Carmi's brother Ira passed away six days later, and less than two months after that, on December 15, his brother Asahela died. Over the next year or so, Carmi began a short-lived career in teaching and attended Ohio University on an irregular basis. He eventually gave up on his aspirations of a college career.

According to a letter Carmi wrote at the age of seventy, referencing the fall of 1846, a happy change appeared in his life:

> In the fall of 1846 I visited my mother's brother, Rev. Isaac Reynolds, who then lived at Racine, Ohio. My cousin Kit [Isaac Reynolds'

daughter] as she was familiarly called, took me with her to the home of Moses E. Sayre, a mile below Letart to get some peaches, and to have a good time with her friend, Lydia Sayre. I suppose the peaches were pretty good, but I soon lost interest in them for the greater attraction of the girl who was so pleasantly entertaining us. Lydia was her real self; for, by misunderstanding a former remark of my cousin, she [Lydia] thought I was married; therefore, there was nothing artificial about her.

When we returned to Racine, I asked many carefully-guarded questions about the girl I saw under the peach tree, and the family of which she was a part. My aunt said that the girl was worth her weight in gold, and I thought she told the truth. Visions of future happiness took the place of sleep most of the night, and in the morning I asked my uncle [Isaac Reynolds] if he thought I could get a school at Letart. He said he thought I could, and gave me an introduction to the directors, with whom I engaged for a 4 months' school, after Lydia had given me to understand she was willing to form an acquaintance.

And on the 6th of May [1847] following 8 months after our first meeting, she became my wife. I have never doubted the hand of Providence in this love affair. The love that began under a peach tree, more than fifty years ago, has increased in power and we think will not only endure to end life's journey, but be more intense and enjoyable when we meet in the Paradise of God.

After marrying Lydia, Carmi began a life as a merchant in Letart, which lasted for twelve years. At this time, shopkeepers had to travel to get their merchandise because traveling salespeople and sample shipments didn't exist. No railroad was anywhere near Letart, and steamboats could go months without running due to water conditions. On top of these hurdles, the closest bank was in Pomeroy and most currency exchanged at the time was silver and gold. However, Carmi was determined to bring the best goods possible to Letart. Traveling east to Baltimore, buying large stocks of goods and shipping them by rail to Wheeling, and later to Parkersburg, was made possible with the advancement of railroads. From Wheeling, goods were sent downriver to Letart via flatboat. When possible, Carmi would travel west to Cincinnati and have the goods shipped upriver via steamboat.

After the start of the Civil War, Carmi Alderman was named postmaster of Letart. There were several copperheads, Southern sympathizers in the North, living in Letart who were insistent that Confederate letters be allowed to pass through the post office. Carmi refused. As a minister and a member of the abolitionist party, he hated slavery, though this brought him bitter persecution. Eventually, his refusal to pass these letters resulted in threats and a plot to take his life. After discovering this, he decided it was best to move.

Carmi moved his family back to his home in Morgan County and eventually tried to open a business in Steubenville, Jefferson County, Ohio. As an abolitionist, and with his rigorous religious upbringing, he was led to support the temperance movement. Seeing the number of saloons in Jefferson County, Carmi decided to make another relocation to Ironton, Ohio.

It's noted in Ervin's *Pioneer History of Meigs County* that most of the land in Ironton at this time was owned by "church people," and any transfer of a deed was on the understanding that "no saloon should ever be operated on the real estate and no alcoholic beverages should be sold or consumed." The Ohio Supreme Court eventually ruled this unconstitutional, and it was stricken from all deeds.

Carmi's wife, Lydia, died on August 24, 1898. It appears Carmi grieved himself to death, as he died fifty-eight days later on October 25, 1898. They are both buried at Letart Falls Cemetery. According to *The Sayre Family: Another 100 Years, Volume 3*, Carmi and Lydia shared the same birth date of April 21, 1826. They were married on May 6, 1847, and eventually had four children: Electa Evelyn Alderman, born on August 2, 1849; America Alderman, born on April 8, 1864; Nettie May Alderman, born on May 6, 1867 (Carmi and Lydia's twentieth wedding anniversary); and their only son, Carmi Benji Alderman, born on June 15, 1868.

# Chapter 11

# DR. SELIM DAY

*I*n 2018, Harrisonville Masonic Lodge No. 411 celebrated 150 years of freemasonry. In February 2019, the Grand Lodge of Ohio gathered in Harrisonville for a re-consecration ceremony. The names of the original members of the lodge were A.B. Dickey, Selim Day, W.A. Race, I.H. Hendry, J.O. Clark, I. Irwin, W.C. Hayes, J.P. Bosworth, A.P. Riggs and John C. Golden. In October 1868, the Grand Lodge of Ohio appointed A.B. Dickey as the first worshipful master of the lodge, Selim Day as the first senior warden, and W.A. Race as the first junior warden. After the second meeting, Dr. Selim Day assumed the position of worshipful master. The following year, he was elected to be the master of Harrisonville Masonic Lodge and remained in that position from 1869 to 1882.

Dr. Selim Day was born in Washington County, Pennsylvania. It is unknown exactly when Dr. Day and his wife, Mary Day, née Graham, moved to southeastern Ohio and Meigs County, but it is assumed that they settled around Albany because the petitioners of Harrisonville Masonic Lodge originally worked under approval of Albany Lodge No. 156. Dr. Day received his medical accreditation from Starling Medical College in Columbus in 1848. By the time the Civil War began, Dr. Day and his son Dr. Howard Day were practicing medicine together in Harrisonville.

According to *The Civil War Guidebook of the John Hunt Morgan Heritage Trail of Morgan's Raid across Ohio*, "On July 18th General Morgan sent a flanking force from Wilkesville to Harrisonville. Along this route, many of Morgan's men forged from the farmlands along the way before reaching Harrisonville.

These citizens submitted claims for the expenses suffered from feeding Morgan's soldiers. Dr. Day submitted the maximum allowed to claim, which was $260.00." In 2018, that amounts to $5,200.

Two days later, when Morgan's men were making their retreat from Buffington Island to Nelsonville, the Confederates made their way back through Harrisonville, looting and stealing provisions and horses. Martin Dye was so terrified of the events going on that he began to run for safety. During his flight, his backside struck a post, and he insisted that he was shot by a Confederate. He ran to Dr. Day's office only to find out that he would live from his seriously minor injuries.

In 1868, Dr. Day and nine others petitioned to charter Harrisonville Masonic Lodge. At the time of its founding, there was no suitable building in Harrisonville for the members to meet, so they met in the DeCamp Institute school building—where Day taught—in Pageville, known at the time as Pagetown. In May 1874, the members of Harrisonville Lodge purchased a half-acre lot along Rutland Road, now called New Lima Road, for $100. Due to lack of additional funding, the lodge wasn't built until 1882. It was dedicated on July 12, 1882, with Most Worshipful Grand Master S. Stacker Williams of the Grand Lodge of Ohio and Dr. Selim Day, worshipful master of Harrisonville No. 411, presiding over the dedication ceremony. This structure served the Masons of Harrisonville until the current lodge was built in 1974.

During Dr. Selim Day's fourteen-year tenure as master of Harrisonville, 177 regular-stated meetings and 35 special meetings were held by the lodge. Dr. Day was present and presided over 203 of the 212 total meetings. His son Dr. Howard Day was master for ten nonconsecutive years, serving five times as master with two-year terms. Father and son served as master for half of the first fifty years of the lodge's existence.

Dr. Selim Day died in 1900 and was honored with masonic services at his funeral. His son served as master during the service. He is buried at Well's Cemetery. According to *The History of Harrisonville Masonic Lodge: The First 100 Years*, "[Dr. Day's] final resting place is said to be 'on a hill over-looking the countryside which he so loyally served as a doctor and leading citizen and loyal [M]ason for so many years.'"

It has been said that "any successful organization is the lengthened shadow of one man." If that is true, 150 years later, Harrisonville Masonic Lodge No. 411 is the lengthened shadow of Dr. Selim Day.

# Chapter 12

# BUCKEYE ROVERS

*I*n 1849, California fever hit southeastern Ohio. Several people in Meigs County headed west with picks, shovels and sifters, leaving behind a depression and a cholera epidemic to search for gold. The California gold rush drew around three hundred thousand people from the United States, and this population increase gave California enough people to apply for statehood, which resulted in the Compromise of 1850. The huge influx of gold into the money supply reinvigorated the U.S. economy and brought the country out of its depression.

The following is an excerpt from "The Buckeye Rovers," an article in the *Cincinnati Enquirer* by Arthur B. Harding:

> The Buckeye Rovers crossed the continent to the California gold fields in 1849. There were twenty-two men in the party, from Athens and Meigs counties exclusively. From Athens [C]ounty: Elza Armstrong, W.S. Stedman, Hugh Dickson, Dennis Drake, Elijah Terrill, Solomon Townsend, James Shepherd, William Logan, W. T. Wilson, Joseph Dickson, M.D., R.P. Barnes, John Banks, George Reeves, AsaCondee, M.D., [and] H.L. Graham. From Meigs [C]ounty: Seth Paine, L.D. Stevens, J.C. Rathburn, M.D., Joshua Gardner, Charles Giles, [and] John S. Giles. Fifteen Athenians and seven Meigs [C]ountians.
>
> The party left Albany on April 9, 1849, and, going to Middleport, Meigs County, embarked on a steamboat and, further on, by boats until reaching Lexington, Mo. Here they organized, choosing Dr.

Joseph Dickson captain. Cattle were brought that never had seen a yoke, and a week was spent in breaking them. The party drove one hundred miles to St. Joseph, where, if they had waited to cross the ferry in their turn, they would have been delayed six weeks, so great was the rush westward. Luckily, some of them were old river men, and who constructed a rude craft, that carried them over the river in four days. They proceeded up the Platte [R]iver by Fort Kearney and Fort Laramie, and to the north of the Great Salt Lake, eighty miles. Cholera infested the plains at this time, and for more than a thousand miles west of Fort Kearney, if there had been no trail, they could easily have kept their course by the new[ly] made graves. They had many thrilling experiences and narrow escapes from the Indians. At the sink of the Humboldt River the Indians stole all of their cattle. Then the company disbanded, and each one had to get to Sacramento the best way he could. Judge Wilson fell in with an Illinois party going to Oregon, and he was the first white man at Downieville, on the Yuba [R]iver, where he subsequently took up the largest nugget any of them secured. It was about the size of a goose egg and was valued at $1,285. On September 20th, 1849, the first of the Buckeye Rovers reached Sacramento, then consisting of only one wooden structure and used for a post office. The tent population was about 5,000, which increased as by magic, so that in less than one year it was estimated at 80,000 souls. When they reached the golden land, labor was worth $16 a day, but dropped to $10 the next season. Provisions of all kinds were brought from the Sacramento Valley on mules and sold at enormous prices. Everything [was] sold by the pound, at $1, except butter, which was $4.

Once they paid $8 for a pound of soda to make slapjacks. Letters from the East cost 40 cents postage, and were usually a year in reaching their destination. A man at the diggings was employed as mail carrier. He took a list of the names of the miners and went to San Francisco, the nearest post office, 200 miles distant. On reaching the office, he had to hunt the letters that were wanted from a large pile on the floor. They paid the mail carrier $2 for each letter carried or received. In the winter of '49 Condee and Wilson formed a partnership with two Illinois men, Burroughs and Barnes by name, for the purpose of prospecting on the Yuba [R]iver. There were no towns and no laws, but among themselves. They agreed that each miner was to have thirty feet on the river as his claim.

After staking out four claims near Downieville, Barnes and Burroughs went farther up the mountains prospecting, leaving the others to guard the claims. The miners began to swarm in, and it was useless to try to hold the claims. "The upper two we thought were good," said Judge Wilson, "but the lower two we sold to a party of Georgians for $1000, and shortly afterwards I saw them take out between $40,000 and $50,000 worth of gold dust. My share in the upper claim sold in a few weeks later for $2300." It was a common occurrence for a miner to be worth $1000 one day and be as much in debt the next day from losses in gambling. There was not much stealing in the mining region, for among the miners, if a person was caught stealing anything to the amount of $1 or more the penalty was a severe whipping or death.

The first of the Rovers to die was Dr. Joseph Dickson; he was accidentally shot by dropping his revolver while prospecting on the American River. Mr. Stedman spent eleven years in California. Judge Wilson served four years in the Civil War, and he says, "The hardships endured were trifling in comparison with the overland trip to California in 1849." A few of the men who went out with this expedition returned home with financial gains, but the majority were not so fortunate.

# Chapter 13

# THE FIRST MEIGS COUNTY FAIR AND THE HISTORY OF HARNESS RACING AT THE ROCK

T he month of August brings many familiar occurrences to Meigs County: teachers and students return to school, and Friday night lights oversee Meigs County's Tornadoes, Marauders and Eagles as they duke it out on the gridiron. But before all of that, Meigs County citizens of all ages head to the Meigs County Fair.

The 2017 fair premium on the fair's website provides a detailed description of how the fair changed locations over the years, until land was donated and expanded to what the fairgrounds is today. It also gives names of past presidents, admission prices and additions of events to the fair.

The premium's article also mentions the absence of fairs in 1861, 1863 and 1864, due to the Civil War and Morgan's Raid. No fairs were held in 1895, 1896, 1915, 1916 or 1917, due to financial reasons, and 1917 also saw the beginning of U.S. participation in the First World War. During World War II, there were no Meigs County Fairs from 1942 to 1944, but since 1945, there has been a fair held every year.

In an 1851 weekly edition, the *Meigs County Telegraph* covered the first Meigs County Fair, held by the Meigs County Agricultural Society on Wednesday, October 22, 1851. Today, the Meigs County Fair is still hosted by the Meigs County Agricultural Society, but it has become more commonly known as the fair board. The Meigs County Agricultural Society was established on March 25, 1851. It has been 167 years since the first Meigs County fair was held, but some of the remarks made then can still be of value today, 154 county fairs later. That original article read,

The first Fair of the Meigs County Agricultural Society was held on Wednesday the 22nd in Middleport. We regard this as an important era in the history of farming in our county. It is a movement in the right direction, and though the articles presented were not numerous, or remarkable for their excellence, it will have an important bearing upon the interests of Agriculture and labor generally. It will awaken interest to the subject, and that is the first step to improvement. But it will do more.

It will lead to active effort to contribute something another year that will far surpass anything that was presented this year. Many were deterred from offering articles of real value and excellence by the fear that they might be so far outdone that they would be ashamed of the contributions. They will be better able to judge of the comparative merits of their own articles hereafter. No one should be deterred from contributing something to the exhibition, from the fear of being surpassed, or of not obtaining a premium. The true value of such exhibition does not consist in the amount of premium obtained, but on the thoughts which it awakens, the generous rivalries which it excites, and the consequent improvements which will result from it.

If every farmer and mechanic would resolve to present something worthy of exhibition another year, and would endeavor to make it as perfect in its kind as possible, they would be richly rewarded, and they would afford abundant evidence that all the wealth and capabilities of Meigs County does lie buried beneath her sandstone. The number of persons in attendance, was, we believe, much larger than was expected, which shows that there has been an interest awakened in the subject which will produce important results.

The address by Mr. Valentine Horton was listened to with deep interest by a large and intelligent audience, and was worthy of the subject and the occasion. It was mainly occupied with a clear and able exposition of those general principles which lie at the foundation of all real progress, and with some practical suggestions, which are well worthy of the careful consideration of the farmers of Meigs County. We are unable to give an abstract of it, which will convey a correct idea of the many valuable truths and beautiful illustrations which it contained.

After the address the crowd dispersed to examine the various articles and animals presented for exhibition. A description of these we must leave to other hands. Everything, we believe, passed off in a satisfactory manner and its influence will be beneficial not only to the members of the Society, but to the general interests of labor and production in our county.

In another article, winners of every exhibition held at the first fair are listed. Many of the surnames that appeared as winners of the inaugural fair can be seen in the barns, on the tractors and in various exhibits at the fair to this day.

HORSES
Best Stallion over 5 years, to James Caldwell $5.00
Best Brood Mare, to William Rankin $4.00
Second best Brood Mare, to A.J. Giles $2.00
Best Saddle Horse, to R.G. Cook $3.00
Best Buggy Horse, to W.C. Hoag $3.00
Best 2 year old Colt, to Abner Stout $3.00
Second best 2 year old Colt, to Gideon Brown $2.00
Best Colt from 1 to 2 years old, to Joseph Black $3.00
Second best Colt from 1 to 2 years old, to J.C. Hysell $2.00
Best Colt under 1 year old, to Stephen G. Harper $2.00
Second best Colt under 1 year old, to A.J. Giles, $1.00

CATTLE
Best Bull over 2 years old, to John Stanley $2.00
Best Milch Cow, to Silas Strong $3.00
Second best Milch Cow, to G.W. Allison $2.00
Best Heifer over 1 year old, to Silas Strong $2.00
Second best Heifer over 1 year old, to Silas Strong $1.00
Best Calf under 1 year old, to Benjamin Stout $1.00
Best yoke of Work Oxen over 4 years old, to Obadiah Walker $4.00
Best yoke of Steers from 3 to 4 years old, to L. Brine $3.00
Second best yoke of Steers from 3 to 4 years old, to Joseph Black $2.00
Best yoke of Steers from 2 to 3 years old, to James McGuire $2.00
Best yoke of Steers from 1 to 2 years old, to Silas Strong $1.00

HOGS
Best Hog exhibited, to Jonathan Rankin $2.00
Second best Hog, to Jacob Swartz $1.00

SHEEP
Best fine wooled Buck, to Cephas DeCamp $3.00
Second best fine wooled Buck, to Cephas De Camp $2.00
Best 3 fine wooled Ewes, to Stephen Titus $3.00

Second best 3 fine wooled Ewes, to Mary Titus $2.00
Best 3 fine wooled lambs, to Mary Titus $2.00
Second best 3 fine wooled lambs, to Stephen Titus $1.00

CROPS
Best Wheat Crop, to John P. Stout $3.00

DOMESTIC ARTICLES
Best 5 lbs. Butler, to Lucius Higley $2.00
Second best 5 lbs. Butter. To Melzar Nye, Sr. $1.00
Best Cheese, to Jabez Benedict $2.00
Second best Cheese, to R.G. Cook $1.00
Best 5 lbs. Honey in Comb, to Martin Heckard $2.00
Second best 5 lbs. Honey in Comb, to John A. Eakin $1.00
Best 10 yards Linsey, to Stephen Titus $2.00
Best 10 yards Rag Carpet, to George W. Cooper $2.00
Second best 10 yards Rag Carpet, to Melzar Nye, Sr. $1.00
Best pair Blankets, to Robert Ashworth $2.00
Second best pair Blankets, to Stephen Titus $1.00
Best Coverlet, to Robert Ashworth $2.00
Second best Coverlet, to Robert Ashworth $1.00
Best Bedspread, to Stephen Titus $2.00
Best Quilt, to Lemuel Powell $2.00
Second best Quilt, to Jacob Simpson $1.00
Best Woolen Stockings, to Melzar Nye, Sr. 50 cents
Best pair Socks, to Silas Strong 50 cents
Best show of Fancy Needle Work, to Stephen Titus $2.00

MANUFACTURED ARTICLES
Best Buggy, to Stephen Titus $3.00
Best Farm Wagon, to John M. Cook $3.00
Best Saddle, to William Wallace $2.00
Best Harness, to James Wright $2.00
Best Pair of Men's Boots, to H.H. Rice $2.00
Best Shovel Plough, to Stephen Titus $1.00

Harness racing is a popular event at the Meigs County Fair each year. The racetrack is nicknamed the Rock to pay homage to the sandstone cliffs jutting into the homestretch of the track, as well as the Indian watering hole

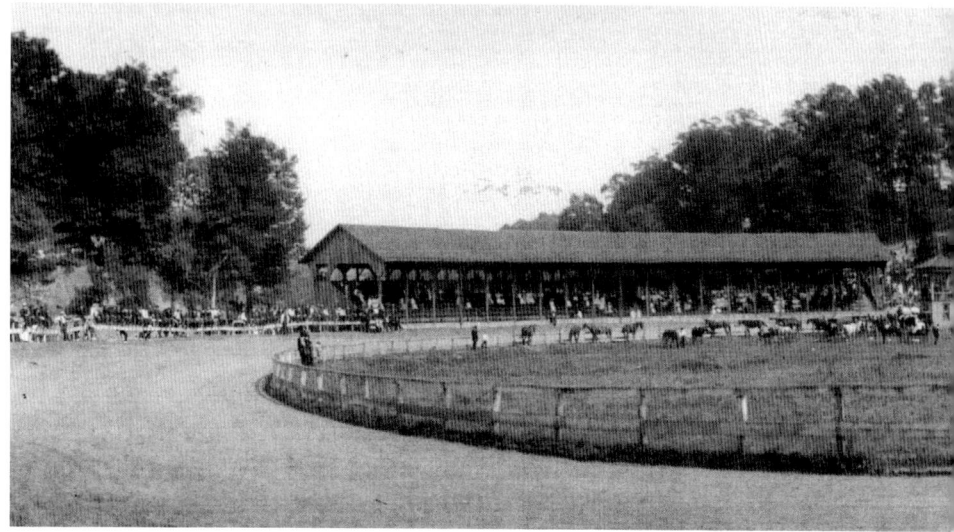

nearby, which gives the community and fairgrounds its name: Rocksprings. If you ask any jockey of the Southern Valley Colt Circuit, they will tell you the Rock is the toughest track on the circuit because of the layout, which resembles a safety pin—one turn is much smaller than the other. The turn opposite the grandstand is said to be the tightest turn on a horse racetrack in the state of Ohio.

After the lack of fairs from 1861 to 1864, the *Meigs County Telegraph* reported horse racing was added to the fair's program in 1865, and it was considered "the highlight of the annual event." This is the earliest record of racing at the Meigs County Fair. Three years later, in March 1868, the Meigs County Agricultural Society purchased 10.25 acres from Leonard and Jane Carleton for $1,500. This was the Agricultural Society's first purchase of land at the current Rocksprings fairgrounds and constituted most of the land that is now at the "bottom of the hill."

The year 1889 saw a lot of growth at the Rocksprings fairgrounds when a tract of land from the Salisbury School Board became available and was acquired by the Agricultural Society. The land in this purchase is now the "top of the hill," where the midway, vendor booths and all livestock—except horses—are housed. When this land was purchased, the upper portion was an apple orchard. Several of the apple trees remained until the 1930s. Additionally, the fairgrounds expanded the racetrack from a third mile to a half mile—the same as today.

The next year, the curved grandstand was designed by Lore Davis and built over the summer using horses and various pulley systems to lift the

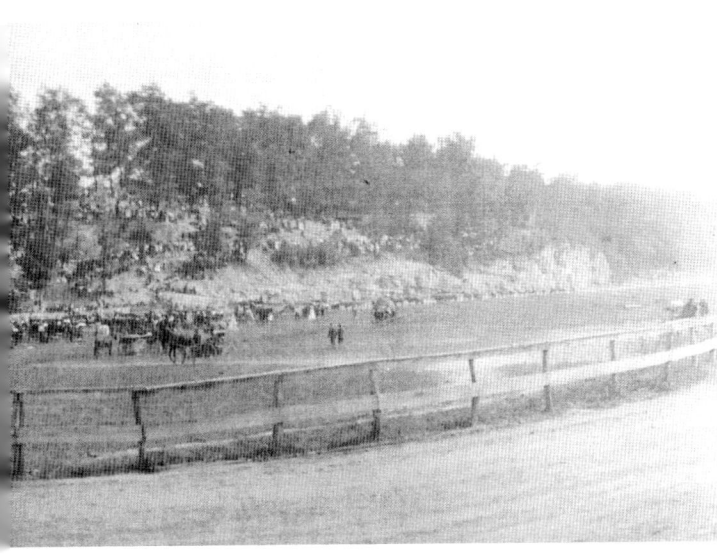

The historic racetrack and grandstand at the Meigs County Fairgrounds in Rocksprings. *From author's collection.*

wood into place. Funds were donated from county locals to pay for the cost of the wood and construction. The half-moon grandstand was first known as an amphitheater. According to the *Meigs County Tribune*, it "easily seats one thousand persons and commands an entire view of the race course. A back view of the grandstand is as attractive as the front. It consists of hash stalls whose counters bristle with ham sandwiches, gingerbread and birch beer." The grandstand features windows on both ends that are said to have existed so race winners could be announced to spectators and gamblers not in the grandstand.

As the years passed, deterioration set in, and to ensure safety, the grandstand underwent extensive renovations. The structure was raised to allow a concrete platform to be poured underneath. The seating was redone, handrails were added, reinforcement braces were put in place for additional stability and a new roof and drainage system were included. Additionally, electricity and lights were installed in the structure, and protective cables were placed along the front to prevent horses from coming across the barrier and into the grandstand in the event of an accident.

The Rock has a rich history, including several locally owned and trained horses reportedly buried along the back stretch of the racetrack. One of those was pacer horse Peter S. Direct who won nineteen races and was named Ohio's leading pacer in 1954. Within the next two years, the colt won twenty-one additional races. He went on to end his career after ninety-eight races, of which he won fifty-three. He retired after setting track speed records at Proctorville, McConnelsville and the Rock.

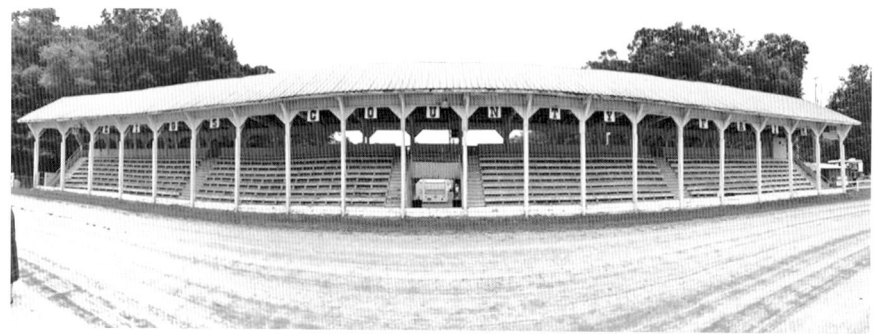

This unique panoramic of the half-moon grandstand shows its modern look. *From author's collection.*

The Spencer family has a long-standing association with horse racing at the Rock, beginning with J.M. Spencer of Racine, who owned harness racing horses. In the early 1900s, Spencer's ten-year-old son, Harry W. Spencer, mounted a sulky (cart for harness-racing jockeys) and launched a nearly sixty-year racing career. According to a copy of the *Daily Sentinel*, "[Harry Spencer] drove one of his father's horses that day and later drove for the late Leroy Eichinger and Sidney Spencer, prominent in racing circles for many years. A notable Spencer family horse was Lady Miller who eventually won at the Ohio State Fair and was trained and developed by John Batey." Batey trained horses for sixty-six years at the Rock.

Don Spencer keeps the tradition alive in the twenty-first century. According to his biography on the Southern Valley Colt Circuit website, "Don is a popular veteran of the circuit. He has a tremendous ability to rate a mile to his advantage. If he gets on the front end, he is difficult to beat. He also is excellent with trotters. Don's father Sid was a legend on the Ohio fair circuits."

Brooks Sayre began training horses in 1976 and started driving the following year. He won his first race driving Salem Spook at the Proctorville, Ohio fair on July 27, 1977. He continued training and driving until his retirement in 2007. As a driver, he had 967 lifetime starts with 152 wins and $234,171 in purses. His best year came in 1982 with a summary of 86 first place races, 38 second-place races, 13 third-place races and 13 fourth-place races, as well as earnings of $68,271. Sayre passed away in April 2013.

Today, drivers like "Flyin'" Ryan Holton, "Choo-Choo" Charlie Schoonover, Jonas Hershberger, Ty VanRhoden and Christopher Shaw attempt to break track records while looking for wins at the Rock. Track records prior to the 2018 Meigs County Fair were held by trotter Victory Tax, with a time of 2:04 in 2009, while Prince of Art holds the pacer record time of 2:01.1 in 2017. Announcer Chris Patterson is expected to belt out his famous "Heeeeeeeeeeeeeeeeeere they come!" and history will come to life at the Rock.

Chapter *14*

# JAMES McHENRY JONES

*I*n a book about early African American education in West Virginia, Carter G. Woodson stated, "There came J. McHenry Jones, J.E. Campbell, C.E. Jones, E.L. Morton, Bertha M. Morton, Benjamin Starks, Mary Wilson Johnson, Fleming B. Jones, Harry D. Hazelwood, Fred B. Smith, L.O. Wilson, and J.R. Jefferson from the Pomeroy High School."

About this time, the article "J. McHenry Jones: 1889 Biographical Sketch" was printed in the *Cleveland Gazette* on January 26, 1889.

James McHenry Jones was born in Gallipolis August 28, 1858. His early life was passed in New Richmond, Pomeroy, and on his grandmother's farm in Lawrence County, O., where he constantly gave evidence of qualities that would in years to come develop into manly and progressive natural qualifications. Being a strong, well developed boy he was put to a trade, that of cooper; working evenings and mornings and attended school during the day. In this manner he obtained a common school education, and at the age of sixteen he began his present vocation as a teacher.

After teaching two terms in the district schools of Meigs County, Ohio, he entered the Pomeroy High School, which he attended for four years, and graduated standing first in a class of seven, the average percent being 94. Mr. Jones was the first pupil of Negro descent to graduate from the above named school. Many have since followed.

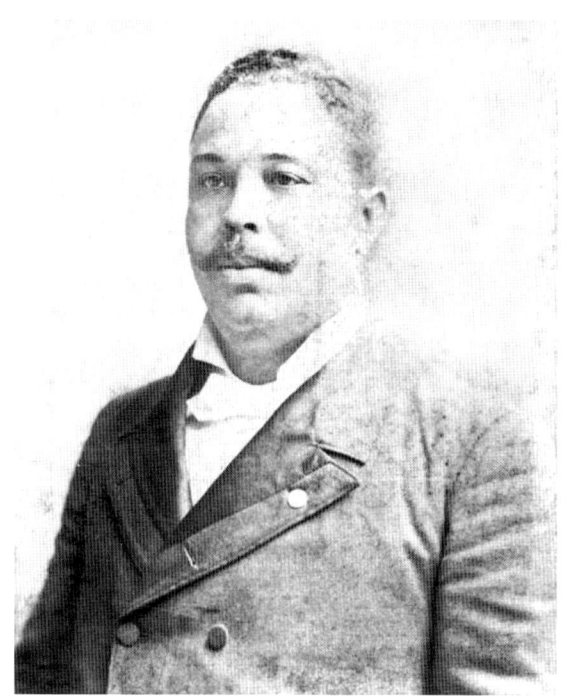

James McHenry Jones. *From author's collection.*

He was elected principal of the Wheeling schools prior to his graduation, having passed the examination in April, and the commencement being in June. He was the successful competitor of six applicants for the position. At the suggestion of Mr. Jones, the school has since been named the Lincoln Grammar School.

Much of its progress and prosperity is due to the untiring efforts and energy of its present principal. He enjoys the distinction of having first graduated colored scholars in the same class, at the same time and from the same stage with the whites in the public schools south of Mason and Dixon's line. As an educator he ranks among the best and his ever apparent good natured qualifications wins the friendship of pupil and observer.

The subject of our sketch joined the Odd Fellows at the age of eighteen years [with] the committee in charge of affairs having obtained the assent of his father. He passed through the various gradations of office, and was honored with the Subordinate Lodge's honorary title. In 1880 when the District Lodge was formed he represented his lodge in the convention, and it never had a better representative. In this convention, though stormy and he so young, he made a step forward that have [*sic*] ever since been a[n] impetus to its onward course. Ohio District Lodge was formed, and from its birth in Columbus in 1880, to the present time, his voice and counsel has been heard.

He was elected District Deputy Master in Springfield, in 1882; District Master in Columbus, in 1883; and re-elected at Dayton in 1884. At the next session at Ironton, in 1885, having succeeded in obtaining the sanction of the District Lodge to his idea of systematic government and the advanced idea, he declined part of [the] honors. The District Lodge by a rising vote tendered him their thanks for excellent management and the faithful performance of duties and honored him with a gold medal.

At the eighth annual session held at Zanesville last August, the representatives there assembled by acclamation again called him to assume the leadership of the Order in District No. 24, which comprises Ohio, West Virginia and Michigan. Mr. Jones was the author of the "Ohio idea" relative to District Lodges. His pungent paragraphs on the inconsistency of the present policy and his strong advocacy of an imperial Grand Lodge, State Grand Lodges and State representatives to the National Grand Lodge which some day must be the policy of the Order, will cause him to be remembered and endeared.

He is a lover of his race and never fails to lend his voice and pen in their behalf. While not a hater of the Independent Order of Odd Fellows he cannot feel toward them friendly because of their adoption of a law that prohibits them from practicing friendship, love and truth with the Negro. Many journals have copied his utterances upon this subject.

In political faith he is a strong advocate for Republican principles. In the late campaign he visited at the invitation of the West Virginia State Executive Committee, the principle cities of the State, was received with high honors and won through his oratorical powers the praises of the masses wherever assembled.

On December 27, 1888, he was united in marriage to Miss Carrie M. Harrison, of Harmar, who for three years was assistant principal of Lincoln School, of Wheeling.

In 1896 McHenry was asked to address West Virginia's Republican Convention, which was held in Parkersburg. This speech served to second the nomination of George W. Atkinson for governor of West Virginia. The speech was later published in the *Wheeling Daily Intelligencer* on July 31, 1896.

On the field of Gettysburg, it is said, that the soldiers wearing the blue and the gray, were buried after the battle in long trenches, one upon another. A traveler who passed over that immortal battle ground a few days afterward, declared that the earth over which these soldiers so gloriously died and under which they were so ignominious[ly] covered, swayed up and down. This may be fact or fiction, but he who observes the signs of the times must be cognizant of the tremors from an irresistible ground-swell which began at St. Louis and will not cease until it rolls incompetent Democracy out of the white house.

I misinterpret the spirit and intelligence of the American people, if by their permission, that herd of wild-eyed fanatics which broke loose at Chicago, ever heads toward the national capital.

The Republican [P]arty is confronted today, as it has been in the past, with wild speculations and untenable theories; but true to its traditions, it fearlessly faces the blatant slogan of error with the gleaming torch of demonstrated truth.

The history of our party is simply a record of the triumphs of right. We were right in 1856, at the birth of Republicanism. Right in 1860, under the leadership of the immortal Lincoln, right in '61, when it was determined that one flag should wave over an undivided country and liberty should not perish from the face of the earth. Doubly right in 1863, when it was finally concluded that the life of the nation demanded the freedom of the slave. Right under the peerless leadership of that matchless soldier, Grant; right in the resumption of specie [coin money rather than notes] payment under Hayes, right under Garfield, right under Harrison, eternally right when under James G. Blaine and William McKinley, were welded in a common chain protection and reciprocity.

We are right today, when against the tumult and above the roar of the babel of populism, we reassert our intention to defend to the last ditch the national honor, and preserve inviolate and untarnished the institutions transmitted to us from our forefathers. And the grand old party will be right in November when it wrings from the red mouth of populistic Democracy, the black, the hissing tongue of anarchy.

West Virginia is naturally Republican. The candidate named was born within her borders. It will not be necessary to look into the misty record of the forgotten past, to extract his name from the cobwebs of oblivion. He is known from where the rugged Alleghenies lift their giant shoulders up into the trackless blue, to where the fretful Kanawha unites with the muddy Ohio, on her restless mission to the sea, from the eastern panhandle to the southern extremity of the state, the name of and fame of George W. Atkinson is a by-word in the mouths of an admiring people.

The logical candidate, his is a fitting name with which to close the century. The nineteenth century grows apace. Already the fading glow of approaching twilight throws its lengthening shadows around us. Soon the rosy morn of a new century, fresh fallen from the finger tips of God, will dawn upon a waiting world. As the purple curtain of the new born century is slowly lifted, and the God of day, his ruddy face dripping with golden perspiration, sends his first fierce gleam athwart the oceans of time, may he discover the union's fleet of states, after a three years' battle with contending forces, moving steadily, majestically forward. The flagship of McKinley, the harbinger, the advance agent of a better day, far in the lead. The twin relics of free trade and free silver deeply buried beneath the rolling wave. Confidence after four years wandering in the dismal swamp of Democratic delusion, returned to fill her accustomed place in the company of her friends, while Hope, her sister, dips her golden pencil in the rainbow hues of heaven and writes upon the emblazoned, the imperishable records of the republic—prosperity, protection and patriotism.

The good ship West Virginia cut loose from Democratic moorings, must be directed by a helmsman trained to the sea, a pilot with a cool head, discerning eye, pure life, strong arm, open hand and patriotic heart.

Ohio County believes that these qualifications are transcendently developed in the superb statesman, erudite scholar, far seeing party leader and Christian gentleman, the Hon. George Wesley Atkinson.

Therefore, in the name of the Republicans of Ohio County, whose idol he is, in the name of the unconditional Republicans of West Virginia, who love him as their friend, I heartily second the nomination of the next governor of West Virginia.

*Chapter 15*

# TURTLE EGGS:
# ONE MAN'S PRICE FOR FREEDOM

*free•dom (noun): The power or right to act, speak, or think as one wants without hindrance or restraint; absence of subjection to foreign domination or despotic government; the state of not being imprisoned or enslaved.*

We enjoy many freedoms as citizens of the United States of America, thanks to our strong military keeping us free. But for black people in the United States, this wasn't always the case. Imagine treading in a bucket of turtle eggs to gain you your freedom.

The year is 1937. Meigs County is recovering from its second-worst flood in recorded history. The Great Depression's effects are still being felt around the country, although President Franklin Roosevelt's New Deal is easing the strain.

The Federal Writers' Project was created in 1935 as part of the Works Progress Administration to provide employment for historians, teachers, writers, librarians and other white-collar workers. Originally, the purpose of the project was to produce a series of sectional guidebooks under the name "American Guide," focusing on the scenic, historical, cultural and economic resources of the United States.

Meigs County's William Nelson was interviewed by a worker for the Ohio Federal Writer's Project in 1937. Nelson talked about running away from the plantation where he was a slave and heading north to freedom. He referred to President Abraham Lincoln as a "saint of the colored race." In this transcription, author and editor Audrey Meighen chose to write in African

American English to portray how Mr. Nelson spoke when interviewed by Sarah Probst, the reporter for this project. Mr. Nelson was eighty-eight at the time of this interview.

Whar's I Bawned? 'Way down Belmont Missouri, jes' cross frum C'lmubs Kentucky on de Mississippi. Oh, I 'lows 'twuz about 1848, caise I wuz fo'teen when Marse ben done brung me up to de North home with him in 1862.

My Pappy, he wuz "Kaintuck," John Nelson an' my mammy wuz Junis Nelson. No sah, I don't know whar dey wuz bawned, first I member 'bout wuz my pappy building railroad in Belmont. Yes suh, I had five sistahs and brutchaha. Der names—let's see—Oh yes—der wuz, John, Jim, George, Susan, and Ida. No, I don't member nothin' 'bout my gran'parents.

My mammy had her own cabin for huran us chillums. De wuz rails stuck through de cracks in de logs fo' beds with straw on top fo' to sleep on.

What'd I do, down dar on plantashun? I hoed corn, tatahs, garden onions, and happed take caie de hosses, mules an oxen. Say-I could onions goin' backwards. Yessuh, I cud.

De first money I see wuz what I got from sum soljers fo' sellin' dem a buket of turtl' eggs. Dat wuz de day I run away to see sum Yankee steamboats filled with soljers.

Marse Dick, Marse Beckwith's son used to go fishin' woth me. Wunce we ketched a fish so big it tuk three men to tote it home. Yes suh, we always had pleant to eat. What'd I like best? Corn pone, ham, bacon, chickens, ducks and possum. My mammy had her own garden. In de summah men folks weah overalls, and de womins weah cotton and all of us went barefooted. In de winter we wore shoes made on de plantashun. I wuzn't married 'till aftah I come up North to Ohio.

Der wuz Marae Beckwith, mighty mean ol' debel; Miss Lucy, his wife and de chillums, Miss Manda, Miss Nan, and Marse Dick, and the other son wuz killed in de war at Belmont. Deir hous' wuz big and had two stories and porticoes an den de Marse Beckwith owned land with cabins on 'em whar de slaves lived.

No suh, we didn't hab no diriver, ol' Marse dun his own drivin'. He was a mean ol' debel and whipped his slaves of'n and hard. He'd make 'em strip to the waist then he'd lash 'em with his long black snake whip. Ol' Marse he's whip womin same as men. I member seein' 'im whip

## Pole Raising.

There will be a pole raising on "LINCOLN *Hill*," on Wednesday next (July 18), at three o'clock P. M. Everybody "and his wife" is expected to be there. Speeches will be delivered, and other "doings" done. It is intended, we learn, to get up a splendid "eclipse of the sun," on the morning of the same day, which will be free to all who may choose to attend. Lest our "Union-saving" friends should think the "eclipse" is caused by the "split" in the Democratic party, we hereby assure them that the arrangements for its "coming off" at that time were all made before the rupture in the Democracy occurred. If they don't believe us, they may "climb the pole," and inquire :

But where, tell me where,
May that "Lincoln Hill" be found?

Oh! Pshaw! Go and ask Heckard, or Smith, or Pfall, or anybody else who lives there, and they will tell you at once.

Newspaper clipping informing the people of Meigs County of a pole raising on Lincoln Hill. *From author's collection.*

my mammy once. Marse Beckwith used the big smoke hous' for de jail. I meber see no slaves sold but I have seed 'em loaned and traded off.

I member one time a slave named Tom and his wife, my mammy an' me tried to run away. But we' sketched and brung back. Ol' Marse whipped Tom and my mammy and sent Tom off on a boat.

One day a white man tol' us der waz a war and sum day we'd be free.

I neber heard of no 'ligion, baptizin', nor God, nor heaven, de Bible, nor education down on de plantashun, I gues' dey didn't hab none of em. When Marse Ben brung me north to Ohio with him wuz de first time I knowed 'bout such things. Marse Ben and Miss Lucy mighty good to me, sent me to school and told me 'bout God and Heaven and took me to Church. No, de white folks down dar neber hepped me to read or write.

The slaves wuz always tiahed when dey got wurk dun in the evenins' so dey usually went to bed early so dey'd be up fo' clock next mornin'. On Christmas Day dey always had big dinnah but no tree or gifts.

How'd I cum North? Well, one day I run 'way frum plantashun and hunted 'till I filled a bucket full turtl' eggs den I takes demovah on river whar I hears der's sum Yankee soljers and de soljers buyed my eggs and hepped me on board de boat. Den Marse Ben, he wuz yankee ofser, tol 'em he take care of me and he did. Den Marse Ben got sick and cum home and brung me along and I staid with 'em 'til I wuz 'bout fo'ty when I gets married an moved to Wyllia Hill. My wife, was Mary Williams, but she died long time 'go an so did our little son, since dat time, I've lived alone.

Yessuh, I'se read 'bout Booker Washington.

I think Abraham Lincoln wuz a mighty fine man. He is de "Saint of de colored race."

Good day suh.

Indeed, Abraham Lincoln was loved by many in Meigs County, so much that on July 18, 1860, a political rally and flag raising was held on Heckard's Hill in Pomeroy to support him for president of the United States. The hill was renamed Lincoln Hill and has been called that ever since. Ten years before it was renamed from Heckard's Hill to Lincoln Hill, in 1850, it began as a community for free blacks. The community included its own school and church.

# Chapter 16

# CIVIL WAR LETTER, 1864

Behold, how good and how pleasant it is for brethren to dwell together in unity! It is like the precious ointment upon the head, that ran down upon the beard, even Aaron's beard: that went down to the skirts of his garments; As the dew of Hermon, and as the dew that descended upon the mountains of Zion: for there the Lord commanded the blessing, even life for evermore," Psalm 133: 1–3. This bit of scripture in the Bible holds many different meanings, including brotherly love.

A 154-year-old letter from the Civil War between two brothers, Thomas and Richard Horden of Bradbury, brings to mind this special bond between brothers. (Note that the letter is written with included grammatical errors, as in the original.)

UNION
June The First 1864
My Dear Brother,

It is with pleasure that I write these few lines to you hoping to find you in good healtth as this leaves me at present. I thought I would write you to find wether you was living or not. I wrot homes several times for your directions but I never got them until I got the last letter. I knowed you was in 2 Virginia Cavalry but I did not know who company. I volenterd in Pittsburg so I would be along side of you. The captain I volenterd under is name is Migraw the eleven Pennsylvanaia Company

G Col. Colter. The captain told me I would have to go to his regiment nd then he would transfer me to the regiment where you was but the captain has not come to his regiment yet but still think I will stay here where I am. I volenterd in the last of March in Pittsburg I received a couple of letters about my mothers death. I am very sorry but it is a road we will have to go some time or other but it is little we think about it when we are in good health. Beesy is in Coalport now. We have a hard time of it here now we have meen fighting and marching all this month. We fit with the enemy 10 days hand running oir regiment is cut up very badely we have lost very near all our officers we lost about 700 killed and wounded. The first seven days were some of us fighting everyday here. William is doing very well at home. Maryhart has lost two of her children, the oldest one and the little Simey, I think is the other one. I want you to write me as soon as you get this letter and let me know how you are getting along, so more at present.

From your affectionate bother, Thomas Horden to his brother Richard Horden, 11 Pennsylvania Pr. Company G, in care of Col. Colter, Washington.

Thomas Horden's letter to his brother Richard Horden Sr. embodied that true meaning of brotherly love. At the outbreak of the Civil War, this man first thought of his brother. He knew he wanted to join in the cause, and Thomas, who was in Pennsylvania, wanted to fight alongside his brother, who was serving in Ohio. Thomas joined in hopes, and with the promise, that he would be transferred to the Ohio regiment with his brother, but luck was not with him, and Thomas was not able to be transferred.

In Virginia, on February 5, 1865, Brevet Brigadier General David Gregg's cavalry division rode out to the Boydton Plank Road via Reams Station and Dinwiddie Courthouse in an attempt to intercept Confederate supply trains. Major General G.K. Warren with the Fifth Army Corps crossed Hatcher's Run and took up a blocking position on Vaughan Road to prevent interference with Gregg's operations. Two divisions of the Second Army Corps under Major General A.A. Humphreys shifted west near Armstrong's Mill to cover Warren's right flank. Late in the day, Major General John B. Gordon attempted to turn Humphreys's right flank near the mill but was turned away. During the night, the federals were reinforced by two divisions. On February 6, Gregg returned to Gravelly Run from his unsuccessful raid and was attacked by elements of Brigadier General John Pegram's

Confederate division. Warren pushed forward a reconnaissance in the vicinity of Dabney's Mill and was attacked by Pegram's and Major General William Mahone's divisions. It was here that Thomas was killed in battle on February 6, 1865, his letter having still not made it to Richard. As the years continued, Richard never heard from Thomas. Richard finally learned of his brother's death through documents from the war department.

Much to Richard's surprise, in June 1882, he was handed the letter his brother had written to him all those years before. According to Pomeroy's newspaper, the *Daily News*, on December 11, 1922, "The envelope bore many postmarks. It had been to the dead letter office several times, but always the post office department would start it on another journey, hoping it would carry the message of the sender to the brother."

# Chapter 17

# WALTER "MOTHER" WATSON

alter Watson, one of baseball's most obscure players, was born in Middleport on January 27, 1865, and was the youngest of eleven children born to Elisha Watson, a riverboat engineer, and Martha Jane Watsonnée Cotsman. Elisha Watson apparently had a decent income from working on the river, and his fortune allowed several of their children to obtain an education beyond eighth grade, which was uncommon in the late nineteenth century.

The 1880 census shows Walter as a fifteen-year-old boy living with his parents in Middleport. According to the March 21, 1888 edition of *Sporting Life*, "Nothing is known of his early life except that when it came time for Walter to enter the workforce, he did not follow his father and older brothers onto the river. Rather, his first known employer was a nail manufacturing plant."

In 1997, *Sporting Life* reported that as a teenager, Watson "developed a local reputation as a pitcher, a positional choice perhaps dictated by the fact that he was 'not strong in base running or batting.'" Another source said rather than throwing hard, Watson, at five-foot-nine and 145 pounds, threw a "baffling assortment of breaking pitches and [had] cool-headedness in tight spots."

In 1886, Watson pitched a seventeen-strike out no-hitter for the Zanesville Kickapoos against the Columbus Browns. The *Zanesville Signal* originally called Watson "Sissy Watson" but eventually referred to him as "Mother Watson." But he also became known as the "Zanesville Phenomenon."

There are several theories about where he got the nickname Mother. Mother was a nickname given to those who didn't indulge in smoking, drinking, gambling, swearing or fighting. Several reports on Watson's character speak of him as a temperate young man who avoided ungentlemanly conduct, so this is possibly where the name came from. Ironically, he would eventually be shot and killed in a saloon.

Another theory is that players said Watson needed his mother with him at all times. Regardless of where it came from, the name arose while playing baseball and did not come from Middleport. Friends in Meigs County often referred to him as "Wal [Walter] Watson the ballplayer." Maternal nicknames weren't uncommon in baseball: the Cincinnati Reds had a catcher, Phil Powers, who earned the nickname Grandmother.

After picking up fifty-two wins out of fifty-eight starts against semi-professional clubs, Watson went on to pitch in two exhibition games against the American Association (AA) championship team, the St. Louis Browns. He gave up only four runs in each game. After these games, Mother Watson went on to sign contracts with the AA Cincinnati Reds and the Syracuse (New York) Stars of the Minor International League. Signing two contracts led to a dispute, and Cincinnati won Watson's contract.

While well known in Zanesville, Mother Watson had to try out for the Reds after signing in 1886. That year, the Reds finished with a record of sixty-five wins and seventy-three losses and were ranked fifth in the AA standings. Watson's audition received mixed reviews from the Cincinnati press. According to the *Cincinnati Commercial Gazette*, "He is beyond a doubt a good pitcher, but it remains to be seen how….I'm afraid he won't last long."

The *Cincinnati Enquirer* reported, "The people in Zanesville are wondering what Cincinnatians think of 'Mother' Watson's personal appearance. He is not a dude, but he can twirl a ball to perfection." Nonetheless, Watson must have impressed Reds' management with his audition. Walter "Mother" Watson made the roster for the Cincinnati Reds in the 1887 season.

On May 19, 1887, pitcher Tony Mullane threw a "hissy fit" and refused to accept the ball to pitch for the Reds against the Brooklyn Grays. After Mullane was "suspended on the spot," and already twenty-five games into the season, Watson took the mound as an emergency replacement for the Reds. He lasted five innings for the Reds before his arm gave out and he was relieved with "Pop" Corkhill. As he exited his first game, Cincinnati led with a score of nine to six. The *Cincinnati Post* wrote, "Watson gave up six runs on six base hits, walked four, struck out none, and threw three wild pitches." Watson's relief pitcher blew the lead, but Cincinnati rallied to win the game with a score of fourteen to ten. Watson did not get credited for the victory.

His second, and final, appearance with the Reds took place eight days later when he started the game against the Philadelphia Athletics: "The Zanesville phenom Watson pitched a fair game but was miserably supported by Baldwin." The Reds lost nine to five, as Watson gave up sixteen base hits. The next day, the Reds announced they had signed right-hander Bill Widmer. Watson was released shortly thereafter. Watson left the major leagues with a record of 0–1, with a 5.79 ERA in fourteen innings pitched. He pitched twenty-two base hits, six walks and one strikeout.

It is assumed that for the rest of 1887, Mother Watson lived in Middleport. In January 1888, Watson returned to the Zanesville Kickapoos, now in the Tri-State League. This would be his last year in organized baseball. His final record for the Zanesville Kickapoos that year was twelve wins and thirteen losses.

After his year with Zanesville, he returned to Middleport and took on a private life. He lived the remainder of his years with his parents and siblings in Middleport and never married. He became a member of the Middleport Volunteer Fire Department and pitched for various independent teams in the area, predominantly Mason City's team.

On Election Day, November 7, 1898, Mother Watson found himself in Gardner's saloon in Pomeroy after the polls closed. He encountered Louis Schreiner, a thirty-two-year-old Middleport post office clerk, and the two men began arguing about politics. Apparently, a few days before this, the two had engaged in a "slight altercation." Around one in the morning, a gunfight broke out, and Schreiner fired three shots at Watson. Watson returned two rounds at Schreiner but missed. Watson tried to make his escape after being shot in the torso but collapsed on the saloon floor. Watson was taken home to Middleport and given little chance of recovery.

Ten days later, thirty-three-year-old Walter "Mother" Watson died from gunshot wounds in the liver and kidney. Schreiner eventually fled to Columbus, Kansas, according to the 1900 census. The *Middleport Republican Herald* described Watson as someone with "a kind disposition and numbered his friends by the score." Funeral services were conducted by Reverend Brainard of the Middleport Christian Church and Reverend Williams of the Methodist-Episcopal Church. Watson is buried at Middleport Hill Cemetery.

# Chapter 18

# JAMES EDWIN CAMPBELL

James Edwin Campbell was born on September 28, 1867, in Pomeroy, Ohio, to Aletha "Letha" Esther Starks and her husband, James Edward Campbell, both of whom had been born in what was then Virginia. James had two older brothers, Charles William Campbell and John C. Campbell. Very little is known about James's early life, which he kept private even from his closest acquaintances. He attended school in Pomeroy—first at the Kerr's Run Colored School before graduating from Pomeroy Academy in 1884.

In 1887, Campbell published *Driftings and Gleanings*, a volume of poetry and essays in Standard English. Eight years later he published a collection of African American English poems, *Echoes from the Cabin and Elsewhere*, well before Paul Lawrence Dunbar popularized "Affrilachian" dialect and the Harlem Renaissance. Many of his poems were written in the dialect of his subjects or the vernacular of the time, as well as Standard English.

James taught in Rutland for a time before moving to Chicago to write for daily newspapers in the 1880s and 1890s, including the *Chicago Times-Herald*. He also became a public speaker and participated in a group publication, the *Four O'Clock Magazine*, a popular literary magazine. Campbell returned to Ohio and got involved in Republican party politics, then became principal of the Langston School in Point Pleasant, West Virginia. In 1890, after the second Morrill Act established land grant colleges for African American students in states that practiced racial segregation, West Virginia's legislature decided to establish one.

On August 4, 1891, Campbell married Mary Lewis Champ in Harrison County, Ohio. Mary was the daughter of Eveline Thompson Champ and Joseph L. Champ, a teacher and former principal of the African American schools of Jefferson County, Ohio, and later Parkersburg, West Virginia. Mary Lewis Champ-Campbell graduated from Oberlin College in 1890 and was also a poet.

James served as the first president of West Virginia Colored Institute (now West Virginia State University) from 1892 to 1894. Mary was appointed as instructor of vocal music and drawing in 1892. His successor, lawyer and teacher John H. Hill, oversaw the university's first commencement, resigned to fight in the Spanish-American War, and later returned to teach.

While visiting family near Kerr's Run, Campbell died of pneumonia on January 26, 1896. He was survived by his parents and wife and is buried at Beech Grove Cemetery. The Meigs County Historical Society erected a historical marker in his honor at Water Works Park in Pomeroy, but it has since been damaged and not repaired.

Following are some of James Edwin Campbell's poems. Some are written in Standard English and others are written in Affrilachian dialect:

SERENADE SONG
Hist, Dolores, I am coming,
Gently my guitar I'm thrumming,
'Neath thy casement softly humming,
Dolores, O, carissima!
All the world but me is sleeping,
Nothing but the stars is peeping,
Up to thee my soul is leaping,
Dolores, O, carissima!

Rise, and wide thy shutter flinging,
List, O list, my soul is singing,
All my soul to love's time swinging,
Dolores, O, carissima!
Outward from thy casement leaning,
Turn thine eyes upon me beaming,
Twin stars thro' the darkness gleaming,
Dolores, O, carissima!

Nightly 'neath thy casement singing,
All my soul with passion ringing,
Up to thee my soul I'm flinging,
Dolores, O, carissima!
Thro' the summer's roses hoping,
Thro' the autumn's dead leaves groping,
Where the vine's dead leaves are dropping,
Dolores, O, carissima!

Still, my love, O still thou'rt sleeping,
While my soul for thee is weeping,
While Love's hand the strings is sweeping,
Dolores, O, carissima!
When, O, when, this long sleep breaking,
Will thy love, to life awaking,
On thy lips my kisses taking,
Know thy lover, me, Francisco?

A Love Dream
I know 'twas a dream, yet sweet was the theme,
And I strive to recall its splendor—
My soul upward leaps as Thought backward sweeps
To my dream so warm and so tender.

Where sea billows toss 'neath the bright Southern cross,
By the sea lay I idly dreaming,
While the stars burned a way from Night unto Day
And the waves like helmets were gleaming.

A maid came and stood at the neck of the wood
And her locks on the Night were streaming,
She was tall as pines that rock in the winds,
And her eyes like Orion were gleaming.

She came to me there and caught up her hair
And spread it a mantle above me—
O my soul grew sick and the hot air thick
As she whispered: "Come sweet, now love me."

I kissed the red mouth of th' passionate South,
Till my lips with kissing grew husky,
I looked in the eyes that were storm-charged skies,
'Neath the cloud of her thick locks dusky.

Then up the Day came with cohorts of flame
And the Soul of the South Wind left me,
And Joy fled away with the Rise of the Day,
For Day, of my Love had bereft me.

I know 'twas a dream, yet sweet was the theme,
And I strive to recall its splendor—
My soul upward leaps as Thought backward sweeps
To my dream so warm and so tender.

OH SWEETHEART SWEET
O, sweetheart, sweet of the Long Ago,
Maid of the blue, blue eyes;
You went one day like a Spring-time snow
And you left me here, ah, long ago,
To dream of you there in Paradise,
My sweetheart, sweet of the Long Ago.

O, sweetheart, sweet, so long are the years,
Filled with a sad, sad pain;
There's little of laughter, much of tears,
So weak are hopes, so strong are the fears,
So much of loss, so little of gain
In the harvest of all the years!

But through my pain and thro' all my tears
One thing, sweetheart, I know:
When done with all the long, dreary years,
And shed the last of Life's bitter tears,
I shall find you, my sweetheart, I know.
Then shall I forget all the toilful years
And drown in the sea of love my fears,
My sweetheart, sweet of the Long Ago!

Negro Serenade

O, de light-bugs glimmer down de lane,
Merlindy! Merlindy!
O, de whip'-will callin' notes ur pain—
Merlindy, O, Merlindy!
O, honey lub, my turkle dub,
Doan' you hyuh my bawnjerringin',
While de night-dew falls an' de ho'n owl calls
By de ol' ba'n gate Isesingin'.

O, Miss 'Lindy, doan' you hyuh me chil',
Merlindy! Merlindy!
My lub fur you des dribe me wil'—
Merlindy, O, Merlindy!
I'll sing dis night twel broad day-light,
Ur bu's' my froatwidtryin',
'Less you come down, Miss 'Lindy Brown,
An' stops dis ha'tf'umsighin'!

Winter Tired

I wus a settin' by my winder
Lookin' out the other day,
On the Airth all white with snowdrifts—
Look you ever which-a-way;
An' while it all wus cleanly
Like a soul that's washed from sin,
I could not help a longin'
Fur the robins an' the green.

I am tired of all this sollum white,
Bare boughs an' tongueless brook;
The Airth is like a shrouded corpse
No matter whur I look.
O, I want to see the robins
An' hear the bluebirds sing,
An' in the pon' below the barn
The bullfrog swear its Spring!

I want to see white turn to brown,
An' then the brown turn green,
The hillsides put their mournin' off
As fifty times I've seen.
O, I want to hear that tongue-tied brook
Go singin' on its way,
Ashoutin' as it runs along:
"The robins 've come to stay!"

To read more of James Edwin Campbell's poetry, visit My Poetic Side online.

*Chapter 19*

# THE COLUMBIA TOWNSHIP
# TORNADO OF 1886

When someone thinks of tornadoes in Meigs County, they typically think of either the Southern High School Tornadoes or the destructive tornado that hit Reedsville on September 16, 2010. While tornadoes can occur at any time of the year, Ohio's peak tornado season is April through July. In 2017, there were thirty-nine confirmed tornadoes in Ohio, and an additional tornado outbreak on November 5 resulted in seventeen tornadoes in Ohio alone.

According to Ohio History Central,

> May 1886 was a deadly month in Ohio weather. Floods killed 28 people at Xenia on May 12, and two days later, from late on the night of May 14 into the early morning of May 15, 1886, Ohio's deadliest tornado outbreak of the 19th century occurred. Early reports were of a single 110-mile tornado path, but later research showed it to be three separate tornadoes. The destruction was impressive and prompted the *Cleveland Plain Dealer* to proclaim that nothing like it has ever been known in the history of Ohio.

At around 10:00 p.m., the first tornado entered Ohio north of Fort Recovery and ended near Celina in Mercer County. Six people were killed as farmhouses were leveled along the path. Three churches and a school were blown down. The next tornado touched down at 11:20 p.m. at Dunkirk in Hardin County and traveled twenty miles into Wyandot County, south of

Cary. This tornado leveled a brick school, dozens of farmhouses and many barns. Eleven people were killed near Dunkirk and Cary. The third tornado touched down at midnight, west of Attica in Seneca County. There were no deaths, but a gravestone was lifted and flung against a barn a quarter of a mile away. Fence rails were driven six feet into the ground, and entire orchards were uprooted in Seneca County.

As reported in the *Telegraph*, a Meigs County newspaper from the time, and later in the book *The Harris History*, on May 12, 1886, at 11:00 p.m., two dark clouds were seen approaching each other from the north and south. They met with a terrific roar of concussion. The clouds joined and seemed to fall to the earth, moving with high speed and relentless fury. The first house struck was a log building occupied by John Quincy Adams and his seven family members. The house was demolished, but the occupants escaped injury.

The former Howery Store, which stands along State Route 143 and the railroad tracks in Carpenter, still has marks from the tornado. The building was owned by Noah Stout at the time, and it was used as a store that was about half the size as it is today. The building was torn off its foundation, the roof was blown away and all the timbers were twisted. Two young women were asleep in the apartment above the store, and when the roof came off, it is said that the women remained asleep and did not awaken until they felt the rain following the tornado.

Next in the path of the storm were the barn and sheep houses of Mr. Gregory, then a schoolhouse. Farther on, the upper story of E. Foster's dwelling was torn off, then more barns were hit until the tornado narrowed to a track of no more than three hundred yards in width and kept near the ground. Nathan Vail's new house was badly shaken, and another house was torn down. The upper story of T.D. Jackson's house, which included a large stone chimney, tumbled over the people in bed, and one person was injured. Jackson's barn was blown to pieces, and two horses and eighteen sheep were killed. The home of S.D. Wilcox was wrecked, and the furious storm still went on, uprooting trees, flattening shrubbery, sweeping away fences and twisting oak trees around one another.

The tornado reached over and swept the farm of Nathan McComas, just north of the Carpenter railroad crossing, and carried away the house of Nathan's mother, Mrs. Margaretta McComas. Margaretta and her ten-year-old granddaughter were sleeping in one room, and her grandson, twenty-year-old Hathiman McComas, was sleeping in another room. Everything was swept from its place—the houses and granaries were all destroyed.

Nathan McComas ran to his mother's place as soon as possible and first found the little girl, who eventually recovered consciousness. Margaretta was found fifty yards south, stripped of clothing and dead. Hathiman lay dead in another direction, with a broken neck and both legs mangled and broken.

Many cattle, horses and sheep were killed. A fine orchard that belonged to J.L. Carpenter was leveled. The depot of the K & M Railroad was cut in two, from the roof to the ground, and carried eastward. Mr. Mort McKnight's frame home was torn away. Mr. and Mrs. McKnight and their daughter heard the storm coming and threw themselves flat on the floor, face downward, and the house was carried away from over their heads. The wind caught them and pitched them to the ground with great force. Mrs. McKnight had two ribs broken and Mr. McKnight was badly bruised, but they succeeded with great difficulty in reaching the house of Dr. Dudgeon, a neighbor who had escaped the tornado.

Mr. Jewell's blacksmith shop was cleared of all its fixtures as the wind retained its strength, and the combination of the blacksmithing materials and wind tore a lot of standing timber, which had the tops cut out at an angle of thirty degrees from the base. The storm lasted about two hours, but the havoc was the work of a few minutes.

# Chapter 20

# W.G. SIBLEY

Two of Meigs County's most famous writers are Ambrose Bierce and James Edwin Campbell. While both wrote incredible works, W.G. Sibley of Racine has an interesting life story as not only a local and national journalist but also as an author of several books.

William Giddings Sibley was born February 29, 1860, and died January 30, 1935. While he lived to the age of seventy-four, he was only able to celebrate the anniversary of his birth eighteen times, as he was born on leap day. As a young man, he enrolled in Marietta College and graduated in 1881. Sibley went on to establish the Hiram L. Sibley Fund at Marietta College in memory of his father, Judge Hiram L. Sibley. The income from the fund was used to support the acquisition of information resources for the college. Marietta College eventually honored Sibley with both an honorary master of arts degree and honorary doctorate of humanities degree. He also served as captain and quartermaster of the seventh regiment of the Ohio national guard in 1902 and 1903. Around this point in his life, Sibley got involved with the Masonic fraternity, eventually becoming a knight templar and a thirty-second degree Scottish Rite mason.

After graduating college, Sibley returned to Racine and worked as a clerk at Ellis' Store from 1881 to 1887. He referred to it as "the great family store" in many of his articles. Later in 1887, he founded and became the editor of a weekly newspaper, the *Meigs County Tribune*. On top of this, he became the state librarian of Ohio in 1889 and 1890. Sibley remained editor of the *Meigs County Tribune* for three years, until he sold it to a rival newspaper, the *Pomeroy Telegraph*. From then on, the merged paper was known as the *Pomeroy Tribune-Telegraph*, and it was published into the mid-1940s. Ironically, after hoping to get out of journalism, Sibley purchased the weekly *Gallipolis Weekly Tribune* and decided to turn it into a daily newspaper. Thus, the *Gallipolis Daily Tribune* was born and would eventually become the only daily newspaper in Gallia County.

Sibley was well known for speaking his mind. Shortly after converting the *Gallipolis Tribune* to a daily paper, Sibley had this to say about what we would call slumlords:

> Men who will buy up old shanties because they can get them for a song, and rent them to whoever they can get to occupy them, are enemies to the moral and material prosperity of a community….Men who deal in that kind of real estate invite into the community on the one hand, all the vagabond element they have room for and on the other hand, are doing what they can to drive into vagabondism all who by sheer necessity are compelled to live in their miserable huts; for nothing so disheartens and degrades humanity as to chuck them in such cheerless surroundings.

Sibley remained the editor and publisher of the *Gallipolis Daily Tribune* until 1920, when Dr. Charles E. Holzer purchased the company.

In the same year Sibley sold the Gallia paper, he was offered a job in Omaha, Nebraska, as editor of the *Bee* newspaper. After only a few months in Nebraska, Sibley was unsettled and unhappy and returned to Gallia County to be the chief editorial writer for the *Chicago Daily Journal of Commerce*. His editorials eventually developed into a column named Along the Highway, which ran in various newspapers all over the country, including the *Gallipolis Daily Tribune*.

One could argue that with Sibley's involvement in any publication came controversy. This controversy sold his newspapers time and time again, if only for patrons to see his opinions and points of discussion on any matter at hand. In his book *Thrifts of Joy*, he argued against nationwide frivolous spending and national excess after World War I. Gallia County's famous O.O. McIntyre worked alongside Sibley and said of him, "He loved his hometown, its people and its newspaper. As he grew older, he took on the serene dignity of thoughtful years. He had a finely chiseled face, a mop of tumbly hair, turned white, like Mark Twain, and deep-set, piercing eyes. One knew at once he was somebody."

Sibley wrote several books throughout his lifetime and his Along the Highway articles turned into a book after his death. Some of his books include:

*A History of the Rose Commandery No. 43, Knights Templars, Gallipolis, Ohio*

*The French 500*

*The Budget*

*The Story of Freemasonry*

*Morning Dawn Lodge Number Seven, F. & A.M., Gallipolis, Ohio; An Historical Sketch*

*Gallipolis in the Cradle: An Address on the 125th Celebration of the Founding of Gallipoli*

*Recollections of Marietta College, 1874–1881*

*Old Ohio River Steamboat Days; Memories of Upper Ohio River Activities Between 1860 and 1890*

*Along the Highway with W.G. Sibley; Extracts from a Column Under This Title Appearing in the Chicago Journal of Commerce*

*Chapter 21*

# MEIGS COUNTY AND STEAMBOATS

The *American Queen*, a 418-foot-long, six-deck riverboat built in 1995, is the largest steamboat ever built. It is a rare occurrence to see the *American Queen* or any steamboat pass by Meigs County nowadays. The *Delta Queen* is currently in Houma, Louisiana, being renovated and waiting on exemption from the International Convention for the Safety of Life at Sea (SOLAS). Unfortunately, the *Mississippi Queen* was scrapped and is no more.

There was a time, known as the Golden Age of Steamboats, when they passed Meigs County on an almost daily basis. This lasted from 1850 to 1870. However, traveling the river in the nineteenth century was much different than it is today. The Ohio was wilder and more unpredictable, due to the lack of dams, which now help keep the Ohio at a steady pool for boats to easily navigate. In the nineteenth century, boatmen had a rhyme about a portion of the river along Meigs County that was known to be rough.

Letart Falls and Graham Station,
Meanest places in creation.
Little Antiquity in between—
The worst places ever seen.

Thanks to modern dams, Letart Falls no longer has falls anywhere on the river. In S.L. Carter's *Pioneer History of Meigs County*, he describes that the Letart Falls rapids "caused the water to boil and make a grumbling, dull noise, and…the eddy of great power, which sucked in logs and everything with its attraction." Traveling through these rapids was no easy task.

The following is a passage from the journals of the Lewis and Clark expedition on September 18, 1803:

> The morning was clear and having had everything in readiness the overnight we set out before sunrise and at nine in the morning passed Letart's falls; this being nine miles distant from our encampment of the last evening—this rapid is the most considerable in the whole course of the Ohio, except the rappids as they are called opposite to Louisville in Kentuckey—the descent at Letart's falls is a little more than four feet in two hundred fifty yards.

The Ohio River is also to thank for the name of the village of Middleport. Phillip Jones noticed crews on flatboats coming downriver from Pittsburgh, and keelboat crews coming upriver from Cincinnati would often meet near the town he was laying out above the mouth of Leading Creek. There they would switch vessels and go back to their respective cities. Because of this middle location, or port, in 1841, Jones decided to name the new village Middleport.

According to *The Pioneer History of Meigs County*,

> Pioneer travel on the Ohio river, for neighborly intercourse, or traffic, seems to have been done in canoes, while flatboats were in use for the transportation of families, produce and goods down the stream; but when it was necessary to carry on trade up and down the river, keel-boats were employed, until steamboat navigation superseded their mode as merchant carriers. The first steamboat that ever passed down the Ohio river is said to have been the *New Orleans*, built at Pittsburg by Mr. Roosevelt, and which left that port in October, 1811 and reached Natchez, Miss., in January 1812. Earthquakes occurred during the trip down. Few charts of the river were in existence, and the falls at Letart were provided with a pilot appointed by Congress, or rather authorizing the courts of Gallia County to appoint a pilot for Letart falls to pilot boats over the falls in the Ohio river, such pilot to give bonds for the proper discharge of his duty. Thomas Sayre was appointed in 1804 as such pilot.

In 1816, *George Washington* was the first steamboat built that had the capability to go upriver as well as downriver. In Edgar Ervin's *Pioneer History of Meigs County*, it is stated, "In 1819 about the time of the organization of Meigs County, the steamboat age was ushered into the Ohio Valley which was without public roads. By 1830 more than 200 steamboats were churning the Ohio and Mississippi….The second generation brought many famous Ohio River steamboats." The first recorded steamboat built in Meigs County was built by Rodney Downington in 1835. Constructed on Leading Creek and named *General Harrison*, it was built to carry freight on a trade route between Cincinnati and New Orleans.

As the demand for steamboats grew on the Ohio River, the need for nonstop fueling abilities arose. Meigs County farmers would float wood boats to passing steamboats to provide fuel. The former captain of *P.A. Denny* and *Delta Queen*, Captain Don Sanders, said, "A lot of good river men came out of [Meigs County]."

Valentine B. Horton ordered construction of the first coal-fired steamboat, *Condor*, which was built in Cincinnati in 1836. Horton went on to build Meigs County's first shipyard at the mouth of Nailor's Run in 1845. From there, the first boat completed in 1846 was *Condor No. 2*.

One of the most well-known local steamboats, *Wall City*, was owned by various Pomeroy parties. According to *Way's Packet Directory, 1848–1994*, the steamboat was built in Ironton, Ohio, in 1874. It ran daily from Ravenswood to Middleport on the Ohio River. Captain Edwards owned a large Newfoundland dog that regularly rode the boat and was trained

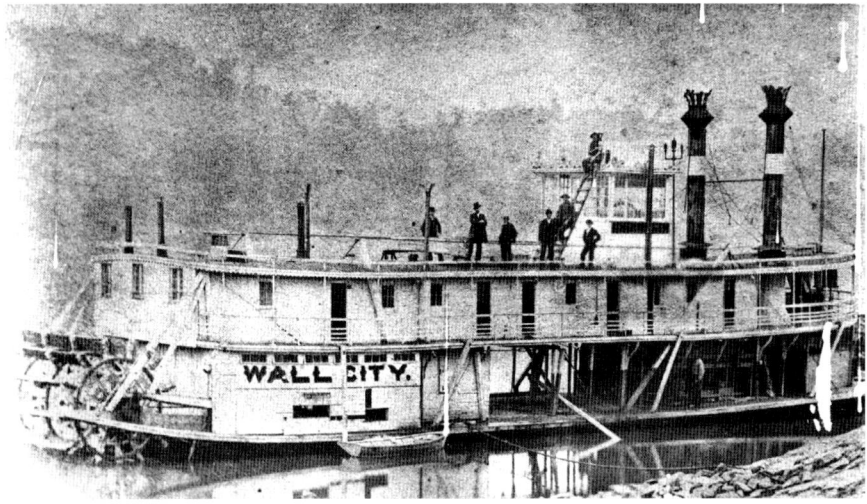

Steamboat *Wall City* at Pomeroy. Pomeroy's nickname was "Wall City" because of its location on the river fortified by the wall-like sandstone cliffs. *From author's collection.*

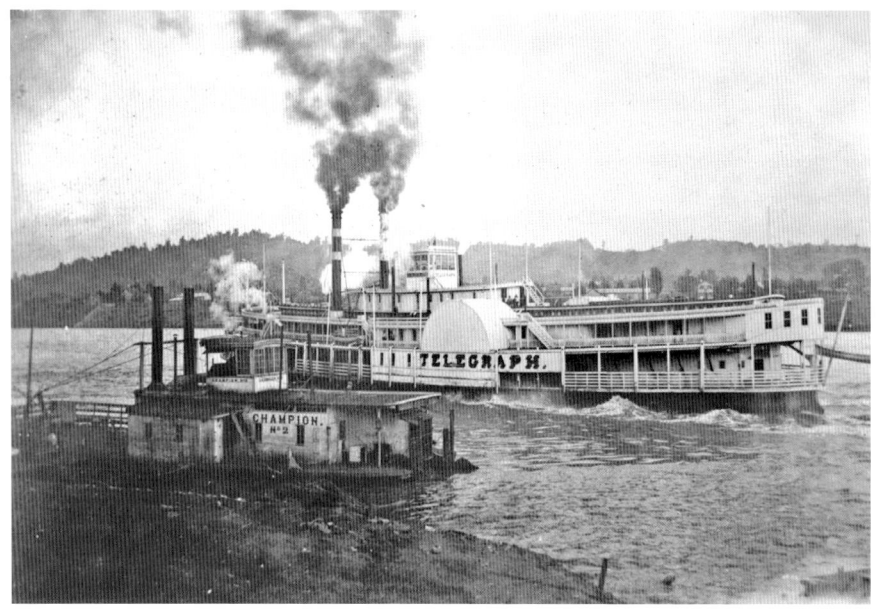

Sidewheeler *Telegraph* with the ferry *Champion No. 2* in the foreground. *From author's collection.*

in various deck duties, such as pulling the lines ashore. After *Wall City* was cut down by ice in 1883, its engines went to the towboat *Marlen Riggs*, and *Valley Belle* succeeded *Wall City* in the trade. Officers included Captain Alf. Day; W.T. Cox, clerk; H.W. Resener, clerk; J.F. Cromley, clerk; Captain J.C. Edwards, master, 1880s; C.H. Crow, clerk, 1880s; and J.E. Wilkinson, clerk, 1880s.

Another famous steamboat that held a longtime speed record was a sidewheeler called *Telegraph*. According to *Way's Packet Directory, 1848–1994,*

On December 9, 1891, Dave Scatterday registered Miss Lucretia Brewer, the first female passenger, at Proctorville, Ohio. The TELEGRAPH made a "fast run" from Cincinnati to Syracuse, Ohio in April 1892. She arrived at Pomeroy, Ohio in 19 hours and 7 minutes and at Syracuse in 20 hours, 17 minutes. She made only one landing along the way, at Huntington, and didn't put out a line there but let a man hop off. In 1894 the City of Madison was wrecked and her roof bell, which was originally on the TELEGRAPH No. 3, was transferred to the TELEGRAPH. On the night of November 22, 1897 the TELEGRAPH was upbound above 12-Mile Island when pilots Charles Williams and

Charles Dufour changed watches. They weren't speaking to each other at the time for unknown reasons. When Williams relieved Dufour, Dufour immediately left the pilot house before Williams had his "night sight." The boat was headed into a rocky cliff on the Indiana shore but before Williams could see the situation, she had run into the rocks and was wrecked. Both pilots had their licenses revoked as a result.

Before the construction of bridges, ferries were used to cross the Ohio River. The first ferry in Meigs County appeared in 1854 and ran between Pomeroy, Ohio, and Mason, Virginia, now West Virginia. The name of the ferry is unknown, but it is noted that it was powered by horse. Middleport and West Columbia also received a ferry that year named *Lark*, which was powered by steam. Pomeroy's first steam-powered ferry, *Kate Howard*, went into service in 1857.

*Little Ben*, named after Ben Redmond of Middleport, ran from Middleport to Clifton, West Virginia. On April 14, 1913, it sank at the wharf grade at Middleport and was pumped out by the towboat *Valiant*. It was later owned by H.C. "Clate" Pickens and ran from Racine, Ohio, to Graham Station, West Virginia. Another of Racine's ferryboats was *Lydia Cross*. Little is known about this boat, but it went into operation around 1876 and traveled between Racine and Graham Station.

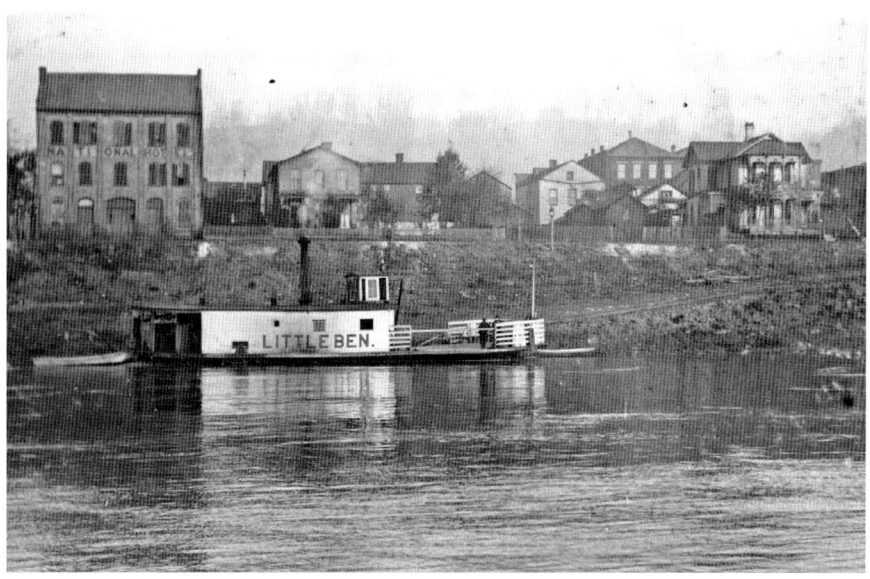

Ferry *Little Ben* at Middleport. *From author's collection.*

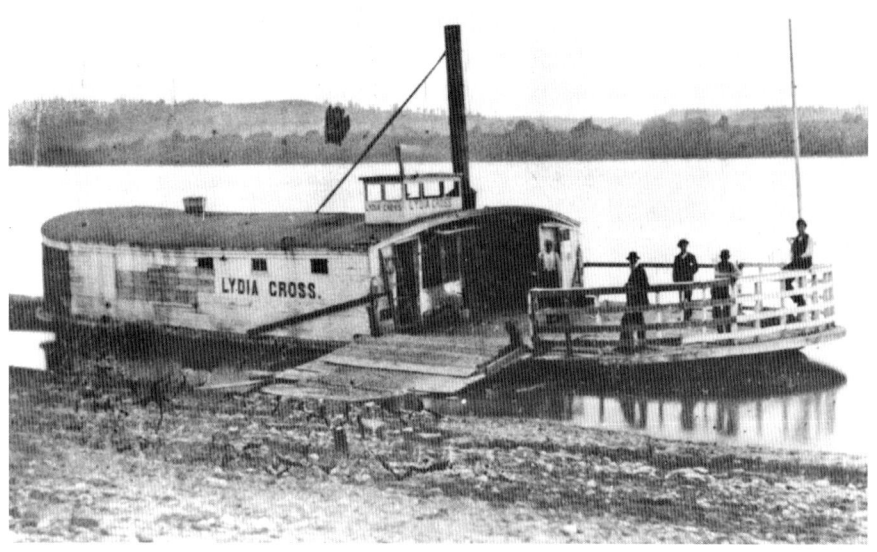

*Above*: Ferry *Lydia Cross* in Racine. *From author's collection.*

*Opposite*: *Champion No. 2* served a twenty-year period in Pomeroy and was replaced by *Champion No. 3*. This was the final ferryboat in Pomeroy and served until the opening of the Pomeroy Bend Bridge in 1928. *From author's collection.*

After *Kate Howard* went out of service, residents of Pomeroy, Ohio, and Mason, West Virginia, were ferried across the river by three different ferryboats, each named *Champion*. *Champion* served until 1882, when it was replaced by *Champion No. 2*. This vessel served a twenty-year period in Pomeroy, and in 1902, it was sold and operated at Gallipolis for a time. It was sold again in October 1904. In 1910, it was completely rebuilt at the Gardner Docks in Point Pleasant, West Virginia, and renamed *Relief*.

The third, and final, ferry to cross the Ohio River at Pomeroy was *Champion No. 3*, built in Mason, West Virginia, in 1901. It began operation in 1902. According to *Way's Packet Directory*, "She ran the Pomeroy, Ohio-Mason City, West Virginia trade until the bridge was built in 1928. She then ran at Proctorville, Ohio and was dismantled in spring of 1935."

Arguably the most well-known steamboat to pass Meigs County would be none other than that of *Delta Queen*. From *Way's Packet Directory, 1848–1994*:

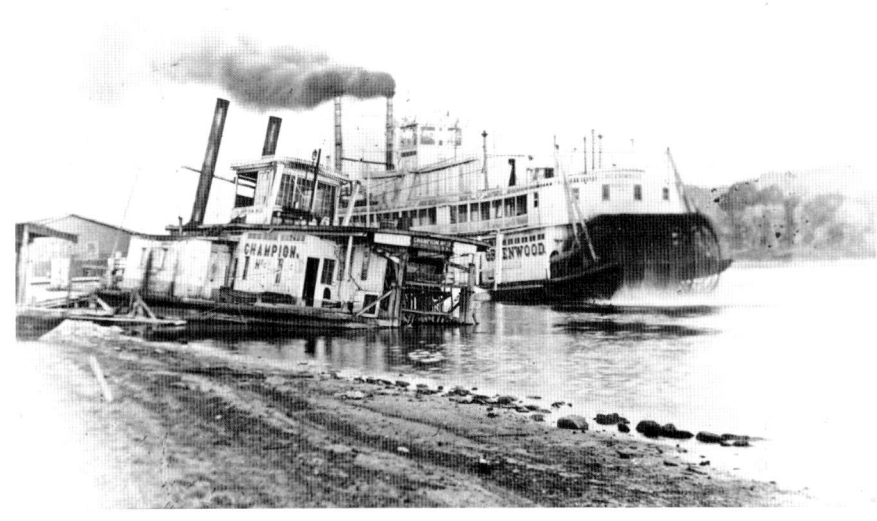

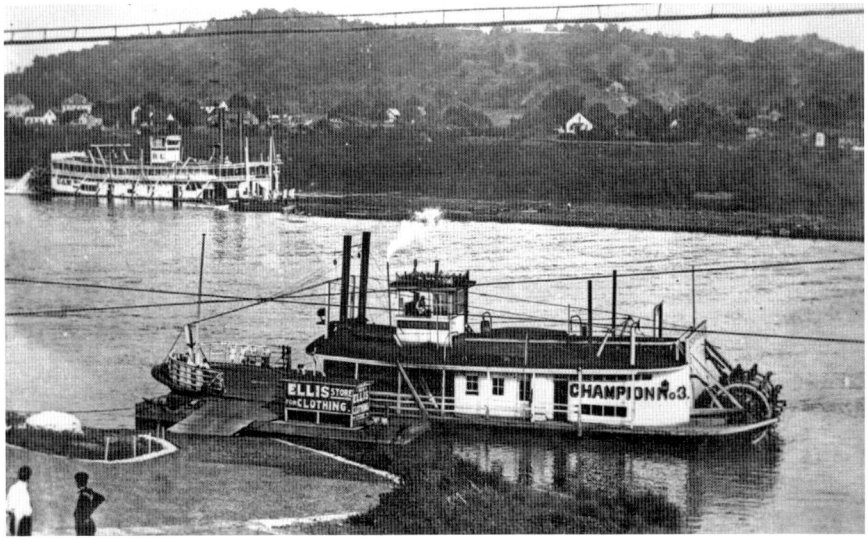

Fabricated at Glasgow, Scotland along with her sister ship, the DELTA KING. All steel work was done on the River Clyde at the Isherwood Yard, Glasgow. Both boats were knocked down and the sections sent by steamship to San Francisco and then barged to Stockton where the boats were completed. The building operations extended from 1924 through part of 1927. Her machinery was built at Denny's Shop in Dumbarton; the paddlewheel shafts and cranks were forged at the Krupp Works,

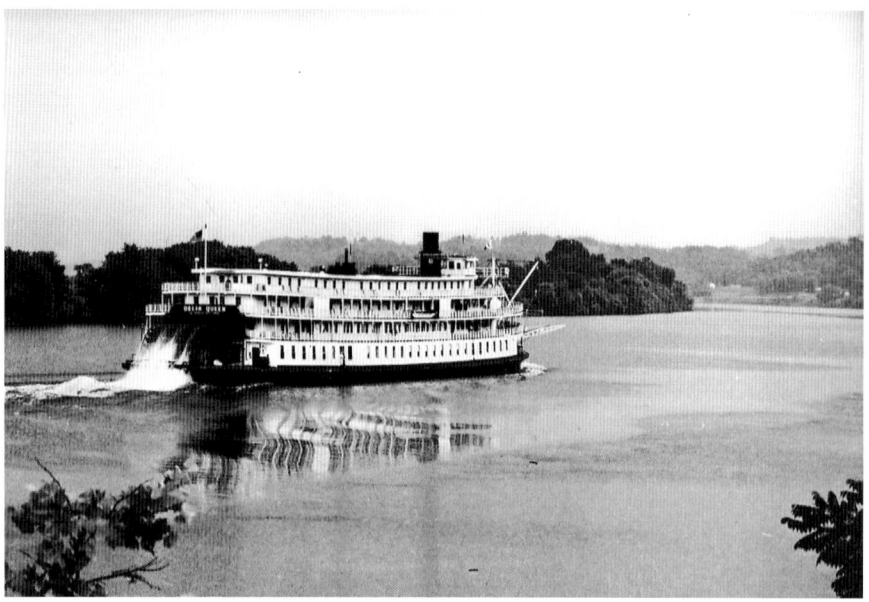

Steamboat *Delta Queen* down bound toward Pomeroy. This national historic landmark has been cruising the United States' inland waterways for nearly one hundred years. *From author's collection.*

Germany. The upper cabins were built by U.S. shipwrights, four decks high, largely of oak, teak, mahogany, and Oregon cedar. When completed the two boats were the most expensive river sternwheelers, costing $875,000 each. In the beginning of her career she ran in the San Francisco–Sacramento trade on a regular year-round schedule. Frequent excursions were made to Stockton. She frequently carried 800 tons of freight. The staterooms slept 200. Rooms and passenger areas were air-conditioned, hot air heat. The cabins were finished in solid oak with natural mahogany and walnut trim. Plate glass windows surmounted by colored, leaded, stained glass transoms surrounded copious forward lounging areas. Seven watertight compartments divided the hulls all hull space usable [*sic*]. The kitchen was in the hold, pantries and dining room on the boiler deck, with dumbwaiters to convey food and utensils. The main deck was built entirely of ironwood from Thailand. Many rooms had connecting shower or bath, white tiled, and twin beds. All hardware was solid brass. The DELTA QUEEN and her sister ship were dedicated at the Banner Island shipyard, Stockton, on Friday, May 20, 1927 and entered service about June 1.

They did handsomely, weathered the Great Depression, but a modern highway linking San Francisco and Sacramento was too much. The DELTA QUEEN's last trip came on the closing day of the Golden Gate International Exposition, Sunday, September 29, 1940. Both boats were sold. After Pearl Harbor on December 7, 1941, the Navy took both boats and used them in the San Francisco Bay area, painted drab gray, designated "Yard Ferry Boats." At war's conclusion, they were turned over to the U.S. Maritime Commission. The DELTA QUEEN was sold at public sale to Greene Line Steamers. She was then transferred to New Orleans, first undergoing repairs and a complete renovation. Changes were extensive. Her two cabin decks were extended forward, dining room placed on the main deck which was formerly the freight area. The air-conditioning was completely renovated; paddlewheel covering was removed; fuel capacity augmented; many new luxury cabins added where the dining room had originally been; new pantries, bar and toilet facilities appended to numerous staterooms. The DELTA QUEEN left the Dravo Corporation yard at Neville Island, Pennsylvania on February 28, 1948 and arrived at Cincinnati March 1 to receive her new furniture, a swinging stage, etc. Since then she has been in tourist service on the Ohio, Mississippi, Tennessee and Cumberland rivers. Following the untimely death of Captain Tom R. Greene on July 10, 1950, the DELTA QUEEN was managed by his widow, Letha Cavendish Greene until advertised for sale. Richard C. Simonton reorganized Greene Line Steamers in 1950 and the DELTA QUEEN became a profitable venture. After Simonton became ill, on November 21, 1969, Greene Line was transferred to Overseas National Airways with operations based at Kennedy International Airport. The DELTA QUEEN ran head-on into Public Law 89-777 prohibiting the operation of wooden superstructure overnight passenger vessels. In 1971, President Richard M. Nixon exempted the DELTA QUEEN from the terms of the law for three years. The DELTA QUEEN was brought 5,380 statute miles by sea, the lengthiest salt water transit of record for a flat-bottom sternwheeler.

Subsequent presidential sanction kept the *Delta Queen* operative until 2008. On December 4, 2018, it was reexempted from sanctions and will return to cruising in 2020.

*Sprague*, also known as "Big Mama," was captained twice by Meigs County men: Captain Henry Nye of Pomeroy and Captain Guy Mallory of Racine.

Built in 1901 in Dubuque, Iowa, *Sprague* was designed and built by Peter Sprague of Iowa Iron Works and used in the Monongahela River Consolidated Coal and Coke Company. Built with a cost of more than $300,000, "Big Mama" *Sprague* was the largest sternwheel towboat in the world with a length of 318.0 feet and width of 61.0 feet. Its hull was 7.4 feet. Its gigantic paddlewheel was 40.0 square feet but was later shortened to 38.0 feet to add speed to the boat. Four 20,000-pound rudders, each measuring 32.0 feet long and 12.0 feet high, surrounded the sternwheel. The rudders were connected to the large, wooden wheel, which was 13.5 feet in diameter, to steer the boat. Its stacks were 50.0 feet high from the top of the boilers to the flutes and were 5.0 feet in diameter. When first built, it had six sets of Hopkins-patented boilers built of a 0.75-inch steel plate and designed for pressure of 200 pounds per square inch. The total weight of its engines was 151,000 pounds. No one ever tested its full horsepower, but it was rated around 2,720.

*Sprague* was too large to navigate safely in the narrower waters of the Ohio River above Louisville, Kentucky. It made the trip to Pittsburgh only three times as a towboat and once after it was decommissioned and returned to the Steel City in 1959 to celebrate Pittsburgh's bicentennial. During its working years, "Big Mama" was capable of pushing fifty-six coal barges at once. In February 1907, *Sprague* set the record for the world's largest coal tow, pushing sixty barges carrying the equivalent of 1,500 railroad cars of coal. *Sprague* also set a world towing record for oil, pushing nineteen barges with 11 million gallons of crude oil. In a 1934 edition of the *Waterways Journal*, it was stated, "Mainly due to the massive tows and cargo she could handle, that were often so massive in size, they caused the Mississippi to actually run backwards after [*Sprague*] passed going upriver."

On October 27, 1934, the *Waterways Journal* reported that Captain Henry Nye of Pomeroy was pilot of *Sprague* all but two years of her service in the coal trade for the combine. Captain Nye and Captain Henry Pawnell, also of Pomeroy, were master pilots of the towboat *H.F. Frisbie* on the upper Mississippi River for some years. When the *H.F. Frisbie* retired in 1903, Captain Nye went to *Sprague*. Copilots with Captain Nye for some years on *Sprague* were Captains Cal Blazier and Guy Mallory. Captain Mallory was from Racine.

Captain Nye left *Sprague* in 1915 to go to the West Kentucky Coal Company. He piloted the towboat *Gleaner* and later *Charles P. Richardson*. After retiring, he returned to Pomeroy for several years, then went to Paducah, Kentucky, where he died and was buried. National Rivers Hall of Fame inductee Captain Fred Way Jr. remarked, "Captain Henry Nye of Pomeroy, often called the Dean of River Pilots, retired and received many congratulations upon his useful career which included making a wonderful reputation aboard the giant *Sprague* in coal boating days."

For more information on the *Sprague*, pick up a copy of Jack Custer's book, *The Steamer Sprague: Big Mama, World's Largest Sternwheel Towboat.*

Over the years, the steamboat era was surpassed by the age of steam locomotives and railroads. However, river travel remained prominent in Meigs County through the early twentieth century. When boats like *American Queen* pass Meigs County every so often, that river history lives on. Judy Kuhn sang, "What I love most about rivers is you can't step in the same river twice; the water's always changing, always flowing." While the quote is from Disney's *Pocahontas*, the sentiment can be applied to life in Meigs County, for the Ohio River today isn't the same Ohio River as it was in years past.

# Chapter 22

# RAILROAD OF MEIGS COUNTY

"Railroad train, railroad train, hurry some more; put a little steam on just like never before. Hustle on, bustle on, I've got the blues, Yearning for my Swanee shore. Brother if you only knew, you'd want to hurry up, too." These words are part of the lyrics of L. Wolfe Gilbert's 1921 folk song "Down Yonder," which has been popularized by artists such as Red Foley, Bill Monroe, Willie Nelson and Johnny and the Hurricanes. There was a time in Meigs County when railroads not only provided a means of transporting passengers and freight in and out of Meigs County but also provided local jobs for thousands of people.

The first railway in the United States, the Baltimore and Ohio Railroad, was chartered on February 28, 1827, and began hauling freight and passengers in 1830. While the first track was only thirteen miles long, it caused a lot of excitement.

According to Ervin's *Pioneer History of Meigs County*,

On March 3, 1870, Gallipolis, McArthur, and Columbus Railroad Company incorporated to build a railroad from Gallipolis via McArthur to Logan—about 62 miles. On June 27, 1876, the Columbus and Gallipolis Railway was incorporated to purchase the above line, about 45 miles which had been partially graded. On May 21, 1878, Ohio and West Virginia Railway Co. was incorporated to purchase the above line. At this time 51 miles had been partially graded. On

May 21, 1879, the line was changed to run from Logan via Gallipolis to Pomeroy—about 84 miles. On October 15, 1880, the line was opened from Logan to Gallipolis and on January 1, 1881, the line was completed and opened to Pomeroy.

In 1881, the railroad was combined with the Columbus and Hocking Valley Railroad Company and the Columbus and Toledo Railroad Company to form the Columbus, Hocking Valley and Toledo Railway Company. This not only opened Meigs County coal markets northward but also extended both freight and passenger services to Columbus and the Great Lakes region. The rail line going north passed through four tunnels between Langsville and Carpenter while climbing out of the Ohio River Valley along Leading Creek. In the 1900s, the railroads operated passenger and freight trains with eight passenger trains making the trip daily from Columbus to Charleston—four each way. Passenger trains traveled on separate tracks out of Hobson but merged at Rutland, making more than twenty-five stops before reaching Columbus.

Section hands kept tracks in order, and crews of five men kept these iron horses running. The crews consisted of an engineer; a fireman; a conductor, who took care of the passengers and tickets; a flagman; and a head brakeman. Hobson became an important point where train crews changed. In 1901, the Kanawha and Michigan Railroad established Hobson Yards as a place for its roundhouse and car-repair shops. Over the next fifty years, as many as eight hundred men worked in these shops and stimulated the economy of Middleport. Although the number of workers fluctuated, they were slowly phased out when diesel power and passenger service ended in the early '50s.

Just up from Hobson, the Middleport train station served the Kanawha and Michigan and Hocking Valley lines. Pomeroy also received a half roundhouse which sat just north of the Pomeroy Bend Bridge.

Pomeroy's passenger depot was on the riverside of East Main Street between Sycamore and Lynn Streets. It was on the bank of the river and was destroyed in the flood of 1913 when floodwaters uprooted the building and caused it to crash into the Remington Hotel. After that, the Hocking Valley and Kanawha and Michigan shared a platform and small baggage shed on the river side of Main Street near Sycamore Street. Ticket offices for the railroads were located in preexisting buildings on the other side of Main Street. The Kanawha and Michigan ticket office was housed in Kasper's Electric Theatre. The Hocking Valley ticket office was in a building on the opposite corner, across Sycamore, and was probably there until the end of passenger service in the early 1950s. The Hocking Valley freight station was on West Main Street just north of Ebenezer Street and near where McDonald's sits today.

In 1886, Rutland received its first railroad depot. The three-room Rutland depot building was approximately twenty-three feet wide, forty feet long and olive green in color. According to *Meigs County, Ohio History: Volume II*,

> The most common room to the passengers was the waiting room with its wooden benches, ticket office, and large blackboard on the wall where the train schedules were posted. The one-cent gum machine was a favorite with the children. The freight room was interesting with a variety of articles: baby chickens, furniture, produce, and an occasional "occupied" coffin. The village was dependent upon this room for all goods were shipped by rail. From the train the freight was transferred to a wooden, flat wagon and taken to the freight room. From there it was carried by wagon to the stores. Rathburn's Department Store, the largest in Rutland, owned four horses and a wagon used to deliver goods.

The last railroad passenger train went through Rutland on June 2, 1951, and the depot was purchased by the Utsinger family for $700. The tracks were taken up and the trestles were removed. The depot was later moved across the street and converted into a grocery store. Its final use was as a home until it was torn down in 2001.

After northbound trains left Rutland, they passed through the communities of Langsville, Dexter, Dyesville and Carpenter. The first tunnel, best known as the Langsville Tunnel, was constructed in 1908 and is more than 714 feet long. Four miles past that is the Dunbar Tunnel, just south of Dyesville and north of Dexter, which is about 106 feet long. Two miles farther, just south of Dyesville, you will find the 300-foot-long Wilson Tunnel. The final tunnel heading out of Meigs County is another 300-foot-long tunnel north of Dyesville: Nicholas Tunnel.

These railroads were involved in several accidents. One took place on June 23, 1911, when a passenger locomotive and a light engine crashed just outside of Dyesville, which resulted in two deaths and four injuries. Another accident of note occurred when a freight train carrying coal somehow jumped the tracks along the depot at Dexter and crashed into the station. As a result, another station at Moxahala, in Perry County, was dismantled and rebuilt to replace the one at Dexter.

The last scheduled Chesapeake and Ohio passenger train made the run from Columbus to Pomeroy on December 31, 1949, and the final passenger boarded the train at the Rutland depot on June 2, 1951, bringing an end to passenger train service in Meigs County. At the same time, diesel locomotives began to replace steam locomotives at Hobson Yards on the New York Central Railroad (formerly Kanawha and Michigan), and employee layoffs soon began. By 1969, only five employees remained at Hobson Yards.

# Chapter 23

# MEIGS COUNTY STREETCAR LINE

ccording to the *McGraw Electric Railway Manual, Volume 12*, the Ohio River Electric Railway and Power Company was granted a municipal franchise for twenty-five years in February 1900. That May, the State of Ohio granted the company a charter for the same twenty-five years. The Ohio River Electric Railway and Power Company owned 100 percent of the stock of the Pomeroy and Middleport Electric Company, which held the contract to provide lighting to the city of Pomeroy. The ownership stock was for the amount of $50,000. Today, that would amount to more than $1.2 million.

Of the streetcar line, Ervin's *Pioneer History of Meigs County* states,

> The Ohio River Electric Railway & Power Company began service on October 15, 1899. With thousands of spectators along the route, Hayes Roush of Minersville was said to have driven the first streetcar filled with officials from Middleport, Pomeroy, Syracuse and Racine, as well as the President of the Ohio River Electric Railway & Power Company, Percy M. Chandler, Vice President of the company, who was also general manager and purchasing agent, John Blair MacAfee, and Superintendent of the company I.L. Oppenheimer.

The streetcar line originally ran from Racine to Middleport, but as demand increased due to the large number of people employed at the Hobson Yards, service was extended to Hobson, allowing a total of 14.5 miles of electric T

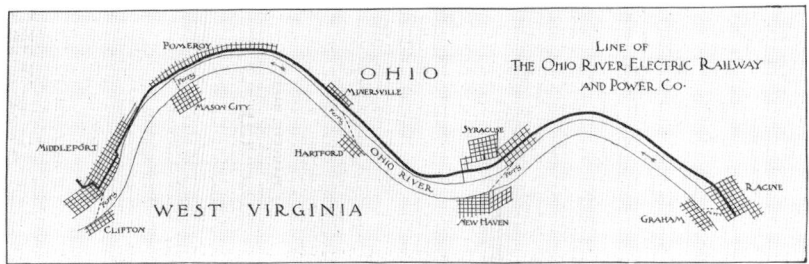

Original streetcar route from Racine to Middleport. *From author's collection.*

rail track at a gauge of 4 feet and 8.5 inches. Eight yellow streetcars originally provided service, but at the height of the streetcar, the total number of cars was eleven. There were also baggage cars that only ran at night, hauling freight between Racine and Hobson. By 1903, profits recorded a total income of $49,558, according to *McGraw Electric Railway Manual, Volume 12.* That same year, total operating expenses amounted to $28,843, leaving earnings of $20,715 for the company. In 1903, a total of 896,083 passengers traveled on the streetcar. The year prior only saw a total of 802,911.

While modern and convenient, these streetcars were subject to various accidents, such as when cars jumped the tracks or scheduling mix-ups caused cars to run into each other. One incident in 1904 resulted in the deaths of two people. According to the September 12, 1904 edition of the *Cleveland Plain Dealer*, brothers George and Jim Holt of Hartford, West Virginia, had crossed the river on September 10 to visit one of Pomeroy's saloons. After they'd had their fill, they headed toward the ferryboat landing to wait to make another trip across the river. They decided it was a good idea to sit on the trolley track to rest. Resting led to falling asleep on the tracks, and around one in the morning on September 11, a streetcar ran over the two men, killing George Holt instantly. Jim survived for about thirty hours after the incident but eventually succumbed to his injuries and died.

Pictures have shown two types of cars used over the thirty-year period. Enclosed cars were the most common, but an open-air car was preferred in summer months and provided many youths a Sunday outing with their special someone—the streetcar, a bag of popcorn and a chance to ride from Middleport to Racine with an afternoon at the Hotel Drake for lunch before catching another car back to Middleport. A roundtrip usually took about eighty minutes.

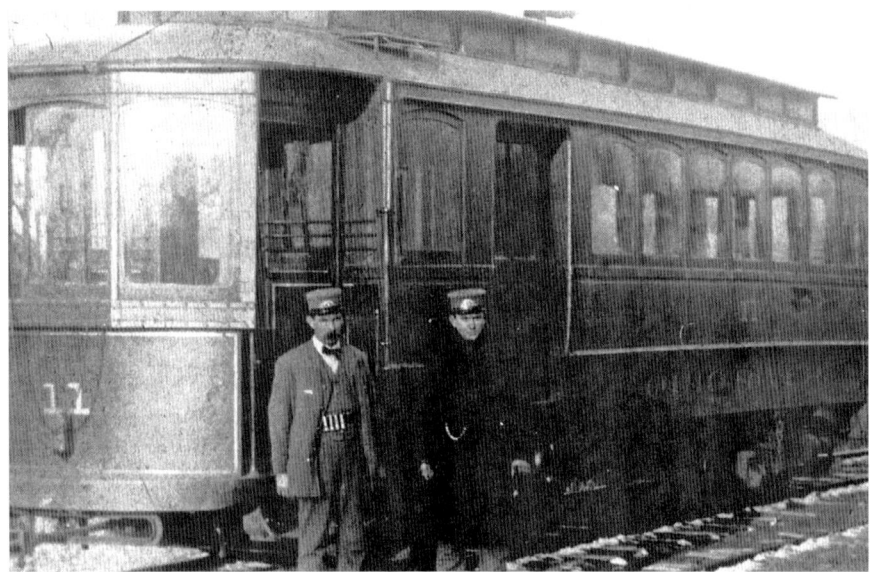

There were two different types of streetcars: open-air and closed. Photograph circa 1926. *From author's collection.*

Miners in Meigs County's many coal mines also used the streetcars to get to and from work. Conductors sometimes had to wear dusters over their uniforms because miners would return home covered in coal dust. Newspapers also show that many people living along the streetcar lines would catch rides to Rodel's Corner, where the Nye Avenue light is located today, and take wagons or stagecoaches to the Meigs County Fairgrounds. Once, on driver Roy Kasper's route, 152 people crammed into one of his open-air streetcars. Allegedly, some patrons were hanging on the sides of the car to make the trip, and Kasper had to walk on the backs of the seats just to collect the tickets.

In the earliest years of the twentieth century, Meigs County roads were navigable only by horse and buggy. A taxi ride from Pomeroy to Middleport cost nearly two dollars, while fares for the streetcar ranged from five to fourteen cents.

The State Highway Department of Ohio was established in 1908—the same year the Ford Model T was released. In 1910, there were still no improved roadways in Meigs County, with the exception of Middleport and Pomeroy, so the people of Meigs County voted to tax themselves to build and maintain roads, marking the beginning of the end for the streetcar line. With the rise of automobiles and the decline of the streetcar, the Ohio River Electric Railway and Power Company was sold to a private owner.

The property was later sold at a judicial sale and purchased by a committee of bondholders. Order no. 3068 of the Public Utilities Commission granted permission for this committee of bondholders to sell the property to a corporation known as the Ohio River Railway and Power Company. This was completed on June 5, 1924. Four years later, the Pomeroy Bend Bridge opened, allowing vehicles to travel across the Ohio River and bringing an end to ferryboat service in Pomeroy. On June 26, 1929, less than one year after the bridge opened, the Ohio River Railway and Power Company canceled its passenger schedules.

Once scheduling had stopped, cars continued to run at the hand of the Pomeroy Salt Association. According to Ervin's *Pioneer History of Meigs County*,

> These roads paid in transportation of freight because of the coal transported to supply its big plant, and because of the fact that the salt plant furnished their additional power to for the streetcar line. It wasn't until 1936 that the Public Utilities Commission issued order No.10,057 that granted the Ohio River Railway and Power Company to abandon its line of rail and was taken over from Kerr's Run [Nye Avenue] to the Salt Plant [current site of the new Farmers Bank] and was maintained by the Hocking Valley Railroad until it went defunct.

When the streetcar stopped running, some of the cars were sent to Louisville, Kentucky, where they continued service for a time. The remaining cars were left behind and scrapped. The only remnant of this era is the streetcar barn that housed the cars. The brick structure still stands on East Main Street between the former Midwest Steel building and Pomeroy Village Hall.

*Chapter 24*

# WEAVER SKIFFS

The earliest record of boatbuilding in Racine dates back to 1822. Larkin's *Pioneer History of Meigs County* states, "Mr. Lucius Cross came from Marietta in 1822 to lands of his own, and started a tannery, built flat boats to send hay to the South, opened a store of general merchandise, erected a mill on Bowman's run for making flour, and sawing lumber, giving employment to hundreds of men in these different enterprises."

The most well-known boat manufacturing company not only in Meigs County but also all over U.S. inland waterways was the Weaver Skiff. Lucius Weaver, whose lineage dated to the Nease Settlement era of Meigs County, served as a drummer in the Civil War. Afterward, Lucius went to Vermont and Massachusetts to learn the monument business. When he became a granite and marble cutter, he returned to Meigs County and opened Weaver Granite Works in Racine. Lucius married the daughter of Captain George Smith and had a child, James Wallace Weaver, who was called Wallace. Wallace's mother died when he was two years old, and he was raised by his grandparents.

In 1869, Captain George Smith started a skiff and boat building business in Racine. He passed this skill to his son J.Q. and his grandson Wallace. While Wallace took to the craftsmanship of boat building, Lucius persuaded him to learn the flour milling business. Wallace went on to become part owner of the Star Mill Company in Racine (Star Mill Park's namesake). Wallace married Lillian Weldon, and they had one son, James

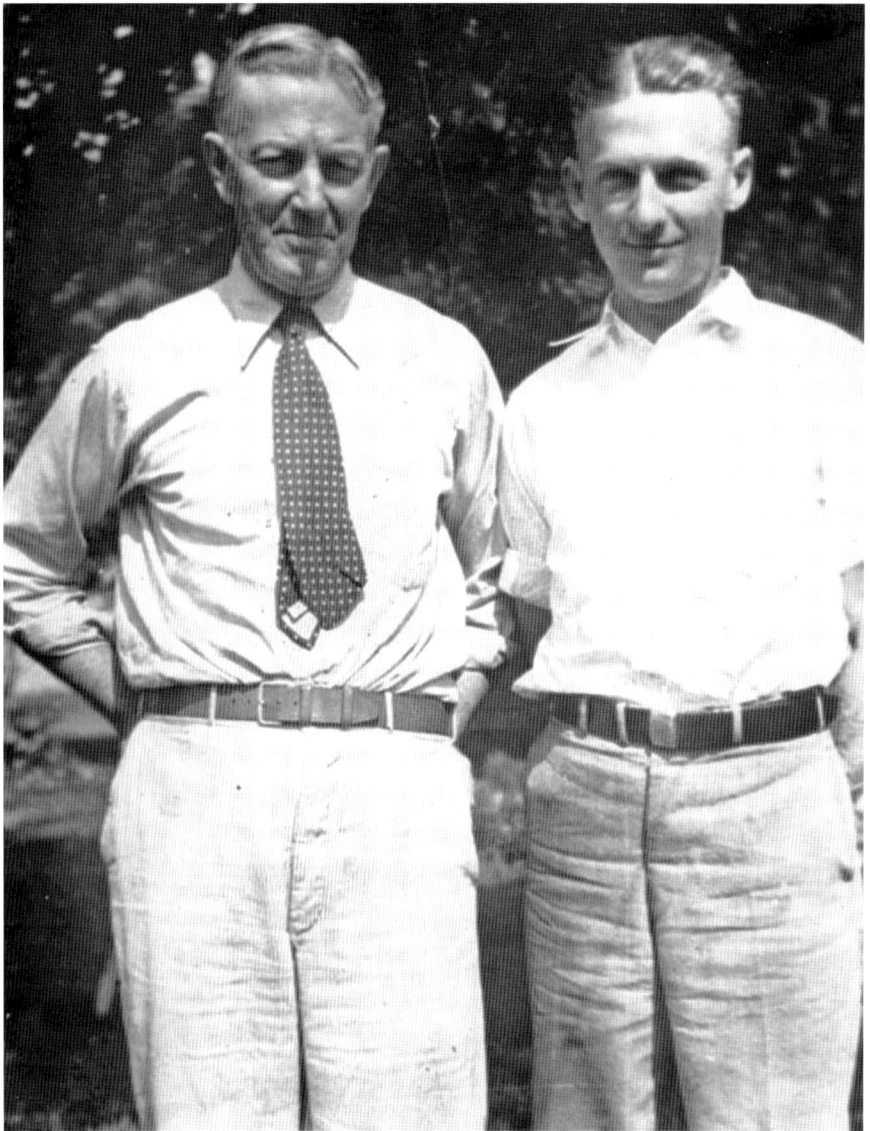

J.W. "Wallace" Weaver Sr. (*right*). *From author's collection.*

Wallace "Boone" Weaver Jr., born in 1897. In 1900, Wallace started his own business, leaving milling behind for his original trade. With that, Weaver Skiff Works was born.

Wallace's son, Boone, earned his nickname because of his love for hunting, trapping and fishing, similar to the famous Daniel Boone. Boone Weaver

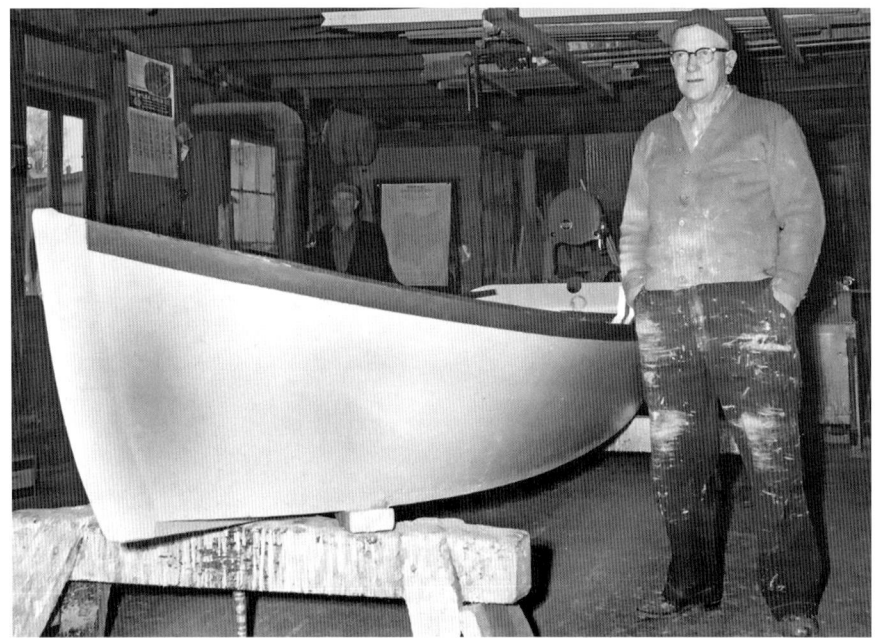

J.W. "Boone" Weaver Jr. standing alongside a newly finished Weaver skiff. *From author's collection.*

grew up in his father's footsteps, building skiff boats at "Creamers Corner" in Racine. The term *skiff* refers to a small, flat-bottomed, open boat with a pointed bow and a flat stern that was originally developed as an inexpensive and easy-to-build boat for inshore fishermen. Weaver's skiffs and johnboats, mostly fourteen, sixteen, eighteen or twenty feet in length, were used as lifeboats on steamboats and ferries across the inland waterways.

The most common woods for these boats were Philippine mahogany, red and Spanish cedar, poplar and redwood, the latter being Boone's favorite. The Weavers used white oak lumber for the ribbing at first but eventually switched to five-eighths-inch plywood due to availability and price. The boats were originally made with hand tools, but as technology advanced, power tools became the more popular choice.

In 1941, Boone married Nora Holter. Eight years later, Boone's father, Wallace, died. At the time of his death, Wallace Weaver was the director of Racine Home Bank. Wallace's death not only left Boone the skiff business but also left him as director of the bank.

In 1950, Boone decided to build his wife a beauty shop next to their home. He moved the Weaver Skiff Works business next door at the corner

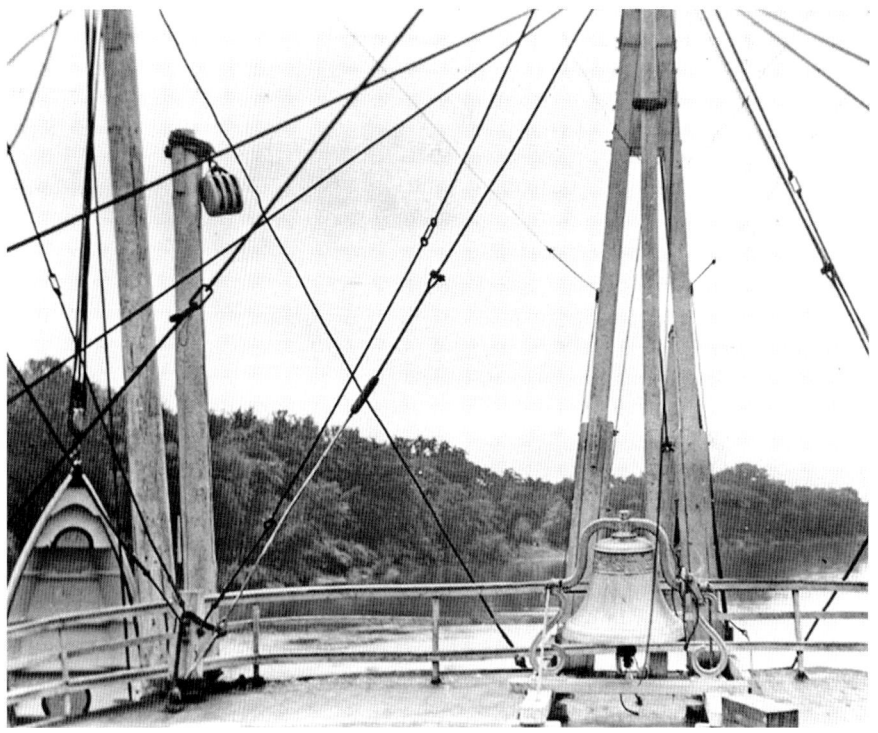

*A freshly made Weaver skiff picked up by steamboat* Tell City, *which can be seen on the bow. From author's collection.*

of Fifth and Vine Streets in Racine. Boone continued to build skiffs at this location and served as bank director until his death in 1978. During his tenure as bank director, he oversaw the consolidation of Racine Home Bank and First National Bank of Racine to become Home National Bank of Racine. The table in the board of directors conference room at the new Home National Bank in Racine is made from a former Weaver skiff. Boone was also actively involved in the Sons and Daughters of Pioneer Rivermen (S&D) organization, which established the Ohio River Museum in Marietta in 1941 and oversaw the acquisition of the now one-hundred-year-old towboat-steamboat *W.P. Snyder Jr.* in 1955, as well as the construction of the current museum in 1972.

Boone Weaver and his father were both active in Racine Masonic Lodge No. 461. Wallace was raised a master mason on July 19, 1910, and served as worshipful master from 1914 to 1917. Boone was raised a master mason on February 18, 1919.

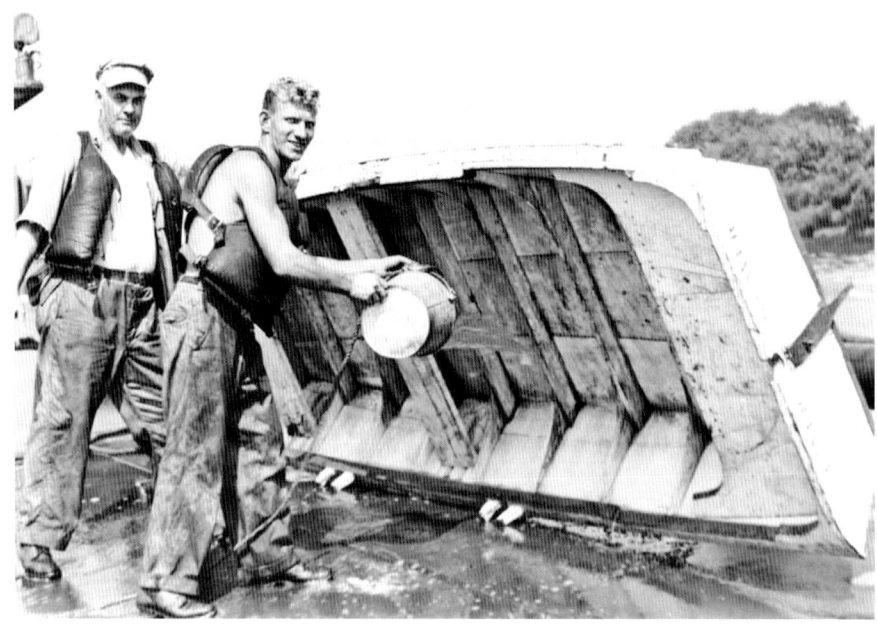

Deckhands cleaning a Weaver yawl in 1952. *From author's collection.*

A year after Boone's death, Weaver Skiff Works was sold to Gordon Winebrinner, who continued the business for many years. Coincidentally, when Gordon was less than two weeks old, he was transported to safety in a Weaver skiff during the great flood of 1937. Gordon went on to build the same pattern boat that saved his life all those years ago. It was noted in *Meigs County History: Volume II* that Gordon had a lot of respect for Boone, and he considered it an honor to carry on his tradition.

The former captain of the Delta Queen Steamboat Company and Rising Star Casino, Captain Don Sanders, who owns a Weaver Skiff, shared the following:

> When the river is running swiftly, and the water is about halfway up the icebreakers, the current builds up in front of them and tumbles through the cement giants in a terrifying display of whitewater rapids. That is when I loved to come racing down upon them in my sixteen-foot, wooden Weaver Skiff, the Flying Fish, and reaching the precipice before

the falls, the oars of the heavy craft were twisted in opposite directions so that the five-hundred-pound yawl spun as it plunged between the massive piers. As thrilling as the ride was for me, and as frightening as it was to a particular passenger, complete control was maintained with the oars throughout the short, but exhilarating adventure.

*Chapter 25*

# SYRACUSE, OHIO: SUNDOWN TOWN

*Any use of racial profanities or language of that sort are used in quotations from articles on the subject and do not reflect the author's opinion.*

Syracuse has a history unknown to many, but most who are familiar with it do not care to remember it. Syracuse, Ohio, was once a sundown town. This is a term for a town that had an unwritten rule of law that no African Americans were permitted to be within city limits after the sun set. Sadly, sundown towns weren't all that uncommon across the United States. They existed predominantly from the end of the Civil War in 1865 until about 1968, although some sources say they continued well into the 1980s. You could also argue that they still exist today.

There are stories about signs at the corporation limits in Syracuse with messages to the effect of "whites only within city limits after dark." Some sources have said there was an acronym below the signs that read, "ANNA" and stood for "Ain't No Niggers Allowed." Still other sources have said that a sign plainly said, "Nigger, don't let the sun set on you in Syracuse; if it does, you won't see it rise." In the book *Sundown Towns: A Hidden Dimension of American Racism*, it is explained that "in Syracuse, Ohio…no Negro is permitted to live, not even to stay overnight under any consideration. This is an absolute rule in this year 1905 and has existed for several generations."

*Sundown Towns* later states, "Intentionally all-white communities dot the rest of the Midwest. In Ohio, independent sundown towns are found from Niles in the north to Syracuse on the Ohio River, and sundown suburbs

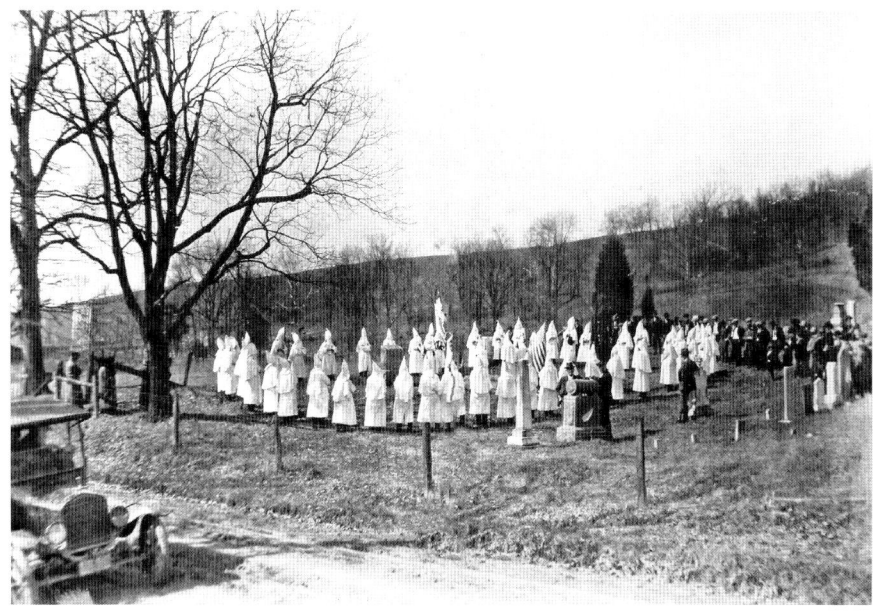

A Ku Klux Klan funeral at Miles Cemetery in Rutland in the late 1920s. Many members of Meigs County's Ku Klux Klan participated and encouraged sundown town activities. *From author's collection.*

proliferate around Cincinnati and Cleveland." The book continues, explaining that Syracuse did not even allow African Americans in town during the day. It gives an analysis of census records for these former sundown towns, and African American populations are almost nonexistent to this day. The 2010 census in Syracuse shows African Americans made up 0.4 percent of the village's population, up from 0.23 percent in the 2000 census.

An article in the December 7, 1905 edition of the *Fairmont Free Press* described how children in Syracuse served as the town's first line of enforcement against black people.

> The enforcement of this unwritten law is in the hands of the boys from 8 to 20 years of age….When a Negro is seen in town during the day he is generally told of these traditions…and is warned to leave before sundown. If he fails to take heed, he is surrounded at about the time darkness begins, and is addressed by the leader of the gang in about this language: "No nigger is allowed to stay in this town overnight. Get out of here now, and get out of here quick…"

If he hesitates, little stones begin to reach him from unseen quarters and soon persuade him to begin his [retreat]….So long as he keeps up a good gait, the crowd, which follows just at his heels, and which keeps growing until it sometimes numbers 75 to 100 boys, is good-natured and contents itself with yelling, laughing, and hurling gibes at its victim. But let him stop his "trot" for one moment, from any cause whatever, and the stones immediately take effect as their chief persuader.

# Chapter 26

# THE BETZING FIRE OF 1917

The following is an article in its entirety from the May 23, 1917 edition of Pomeroy's *Tribune-Telegraph* newspaper covering the Betzing housefire in Minersville in 1917. Not only does the article remember the lives lost, but it also reminds us of how a life can change in an instant.

The home of Mr. and Mrs. Betzing and their six children was located on the riverfront at Minersville, the third building above Windsor Salt Works lot. It was a story and a half frame building of old time construction and odd arrangement. Mr. and Mrs. Betzing and baby occupied a room on the ground floor. Five children slept upstairs.

According to Mr. Betzing, he arose at about 5 o'clock to go to the river with his brother, Pete, to look at some trotlines. He talked with his wife, who remained in bed. He carried a lamp into the next room and extinguished it on leaving the house. He waited sometime on the riverbank before his brother arrived at about 5:30. There was nothing to indicate anything amiss at the house. Nor was there any evidence of anyone else astir in the neighborhood.

It was a calm, beautiful, serene Sabbath Morning with the whole neighborhood enjoying rest, peace and fancied security. On any other morning of the week, there would have been activity on every hand in preparation for the day's work, and possibly the outcome of the fire would have been less disastrous had the neighbors had fairer warning.

When out on a line nearly across the river, Mr. Betzing's attention was attracted by the noise of a dull sounding explosion. In a few moments, he was horrified to see the flames burning from the windows of his home and to hear the screams of his children. In spite of their frantic efforts, they only succeeded in reaching the scene when it was too late to be of assistance. Naturally, the father was frantic and was restrained with difficulty from rushing into the death heap to join his loved ones.

There are several theories to the origin of the fire, although the facts never will be certainly known. One theory is that the oil lamp may have exploded. Another, and the more plausible is that Mrs. Betzing arose and attempted to light the fire in the kitchen stove using oil (or gasoline by mistake) and when an explosion resulted, in which she was so injured the she could neither escape or give alarm. She did manage, however, in reaching the next room with the babe clasped in her arms. If she had been in the kitchen, she probably went there taking the baby with her. The stove was found tilted up on the rear end as if thrust that way by explosion before it was dropped to the ground by the burning away of the floor.

The Walter Thomas family on one side and Grant Hood's on the other were aroused by the cries of the perishing and were horrified to see the Betzing home in flames. Ray Thomas was the first on the scene and made a superhuman attempt to rescue a boy and a girl from the upstairs window while another was trying to force in one of the downstairs doors. Ray was painfully burned and had to give up.

Grant Hood then went up the ladder and tried to pull the girl out, but the window sash had fallen on her and was holding fast. Back of his sister, the son, Earl, age 15, was standing with an expression on his face that he was particularly unconscious. Neither of the children uttered a word. Soon the house fell in and the children disappeared in the flaming mass.

There were heroes there that morning, but the handicaps were such that heroism availed nothing. Those seven people went to eternity because fate willed it so.

Mrs. Betzing, the mother was 36 years of age. She was the daughter of Mr. and Mrs. Frank O'Neil of Mason. She was a devoted mother, who was giving her whole life's activities to her home and her children. The children were Earl, the only boy aged 15; Clara, 13; Beulah, 10; Helen, 7; Eleanor, 5; and Florence, the 18-month-old baby.

The Walter Thomas home, next door west, soon caught fire and burned to the ground. Mr. Thomas has been invalid for months and had to be carried out of the doomed building. A part of the household effects were saved. Lou Custer's house, nest to Thomas', was saved only by a great effort, and that of Grant Hood's, east of Betzing's, was saved from burning by hard work and protection of a large elm tree between the properties.

Undertaker Ben Ewing of the B.F. Biggs Co. was early on the scene and worked hard and intelligently with the help of neighbors in removing the bodies compactly as possible from the heap of burning embers. Not one of the corpses retained any semblance of human form. Three of the little forms found on the bedsprings, indicating that they suffocated and expired without leaving the bed. The two older children were seen to fall back into the flames after an attempt to escape by an upstairs window. The youngest dies in her mother's arm.

The remains of Mrs. Betzing and the six children were removed to the home of her parents at Mason, Monday afternoon the mother and babe in one casket and the other five children in the other. The funeral services were held at the M.E. church at Mason yesterday afternoon, conducted by Rev. Wollard, the Syracuse M.E. minister. It was one of the largest gatherings that ever attended a funeral in the Bend, hundreds of people not being able to gain admission in the church. It required seven trips of the ferryboat to convey the people from this side to Mason.

The Minersville Sunday school attended in a body. Likewise, one hundred and fifty fellow miners from the Rolling Mill Mine, where Mr. Betzing is employed.

Mr. Betzing has been almost frantic with grief, and the entire community shares in the great impulse of sympathy for the man who in a few minutes before his very eyes had to witness the wiping out of his home and his dear ones. It is well nigh enough to destroy the man's reasons.

The Betzing home was insured for $300, and the household goods for $500. Hundreds of people visited the scene of the catastrophe Sunday, which will remain as a topic of discussion in Minersville for many years to come.

The five Betzing children and Mrs. Clara Betzing were buried together in Odd Fellows Cemetery in Mason, West Virginia in 1917. Joseph Betzing died in Syracuse on January 27, 1945 and was buried

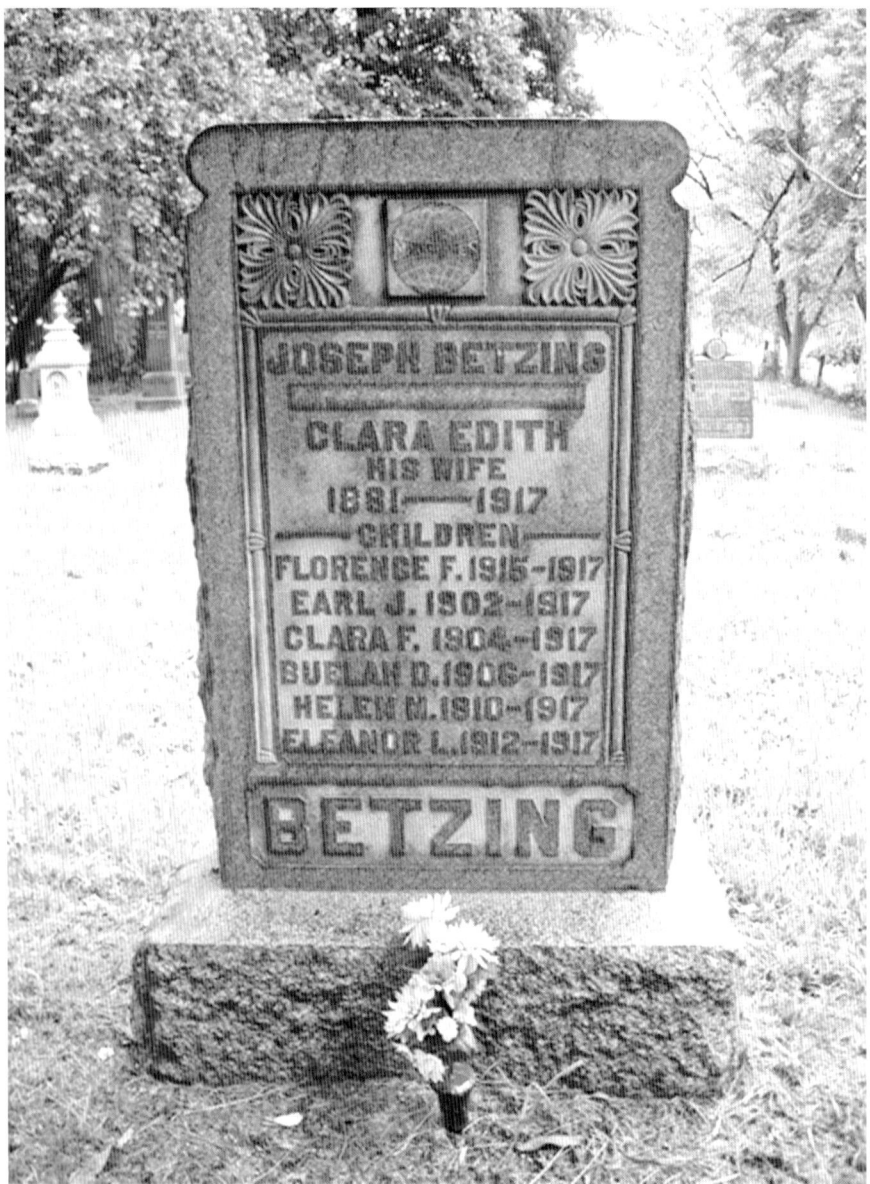

The headstone of Mrs. Betzing and her children in Odd Fellows Cemetery in Mason. *From author's collection.*

alongside his wife and five children that he lost 28 years before. As a reminder, many fire departments in Meigs County have teamed with the American Red Cross to install smoke detectors free of charge. In some instances, departments are able to contact the Red Cross to obtain smoke detectors for installation, free of charge. Please contact your local fire department for more information.

*Chapter 27*

# JAMES BRIDGEMAN

James Bridgeman came to the New World in 1636 and settled in North Hampton, Massachusetts. The Bridgeman family lived in New England for the next 160 years, until Quartus Bridgeman III, born on November 11, 1805, settled in Minersville in 1834 and opened a coal mine. In 1837, he purchased a one-hundred-acre farm in Syracuse. That same year, he married Rebecca Newell.

Quartus and Rebecca's first house was a log cabin along the river. One morning, Quartus and Rebecca awoke to find their son Lonnis's cradle floating in floodwaters that had crept into the cabin overnight. After this incident, the couple decided to relocate to a higher location on their property, and construction of the home that would come to be known as the "Old Brick" began. It is colonial in design with walls that are four layers of brick in thickness.

The Bridgeman family welcomed many Methodist preachers into their homes while they traveled the circuit from church to church to preach the gospel. According to family history, when a scheduled circuit preacher failed to appear, Quartus would take the preacher's place and preach himself. He was said to be an "exhorter" of the Methodist faith. Quartus mined coal, cut wood, worked his farm and carried on civic activities and church duties until 1860, when he died from a stroke.

According to "The Old Brick" by Myrtle Bridgeman-Dunn:

> At this time, [Rebecca] assumed the management of his business and the land. Rebecca Newell-Bridgeman was noted for being a very

gifted and talented woman in her day, and was never known to waiver under difficulties. She was fortunate enough to have the assistance of a fine family, the Johnsons, whose house was located on the corner of her property.

Quartus and Rebecca had six children. Their oldest, Zelda Bridgeman, married John Blair, who was superintendent of the Syracuse Coal and Salt Works. He was a prosperous landholder in Meigs County and was very active in local and school affairs.

Emory Bridgeman, one of Quarts' children, graduated from Duff's College in Pittsburgh. He and his brother Austin enlisted in Company F of the Sixty-Third Volunteer Infantry, which was organized in Marietta. Upon their departure from the Bridgeman homestead, Emory broke off a branch from a newly cut ailanthus tree and stuck it in the ground alongside the road remarking, "Let it stand until I come back." Unfortunately, the two brothers would never return.

The Ohio Sixty-Third served under Major General John Pope in Missouri as part of the Ohio Brigade in Mississippi. While fighting, Emory grew ill and was discharged. After making a recovery, he reenlisted in the Thirteenth (West) Virginia Volunteer Infantry and was promoted to lieutenant of his regiment.

On April 28, 1863, Confederate forces, under Brigadier General Albert G. Jenkins, left from Hamlin, West Virginia, heading to Point Pleasant, West Virginia, and planning to attack a Union fort. A skirmish ensued with Federal troops at Hurricane Bridge who were camped on the west side of Hurricane Creek. This was the Thirteenth (West) Virginia Volunteer Infantry under Colonel W.R. Brown. After five hours of firing from both sides, General Jenkins withdrew from the fighting and continued up Hurricane Creek Road to the Kanawha River.

Confederate command sent a request to Brown to surrender, but Brown declined. Five hours of fighting ensued, where the Confederates surrounded the Federal troops on three sides, using three nearby hills to shoot rifles and sharpshooters. The Union infantry held its position, incurring a small number of casualties—four dead, one of whom was Emory Bridgeman, and three wounded. Jenkins withdrew his forces from the fight and took cover behind the hills before continuing on his way up the Kanawha Valley.

Austin Bridgeman continued in the Sixty-Third Ohio Infantry after his brother's death. At New Madrid, Missouri, the Sixty-Third was brigaded with other Ohio regiments in what became known as the Ohio

Brigade. It took part in the operations that resulted in the surrender of Island No. 10. In April 1862, the Sixty-Third joined Major General Henry Halleck's forces near Corinth, Mississippi. After the evacuation, it operated in northern Alabama and participated in the battles of Iuka and Corinth in the army of William S. Rosecrans. Colonel Sprague was promoted to brigadier general, and Oscar L. Jackson assumed command of the regiment.

During 1863, the Sixty-Third operated mostly in northern Alabama and Tennessee. In January 1864, most of the men reenlisted for three years, and the regiment went to Ohio on veteran furlough. In May, it joined Sherman's Atlanta campaign and shared in all of the battles until the end of the campaign. In autumn, the Sixty-Third took part in Sherman's March to the Sea.

Unfortunately for Austin Bridgeman, he was taken prisoner at the Battle of Atlanta and spent seven months in the infamous Andersonville prison. At the end of the war, Austin was released and was to be sent home via the steamboat *Sultana*.

According to the Library of Congress,

> On April 23, 1865, the vessel docked in Vicksburg, Mississippi to address issues with the boiler during a routine journey from New Orleans. While in port, it was contracted by the U.S. Government to carry former Union prisoners of war from Confederate prisons, such as Andersonville and Cahaba, back into Northern territory. In order to fulfill the lucrative contract, J. Cass Mason, the Sultana's captain, opted to patch the leaky boiler rather than complete more extensive and time-consuming repairs. Fearing that his colleagues were taking bribes to transport prisoners on other boats, Union Army Captain George Williams, who oversaw the operation, hastily ordered that all former prisoners at the parole camp and hospital at Vicksburg be transported on the Sultana. Although it was designed to only hold 376 persons, more than 2,000 Union troops were crowded onto the steamboat—more than five times its legal carrying capacity. Despite concerns of overloading from several officers, Williams refused to divide the men, insisting that they travel on one vessel.

The *Sultana* steamed north on the Mississippi River, but severe overcrowding and faster river currents caused by the spring thaw put increased pressure on its newly patched boilers. Shortly after leaving Memphis, Tennessee, on April 27, the overstrained boilers exploded, blowing apart the center of the boat and starting an uncontrollable fire. Many of those who were not killed immediately perished as they tried to swim to shore. Of the initial survivors, two hundred later died from burns sustained during the incident. Records indicate that eighteen hundred men died, making the *Sultana* incident the deadliest maritime disaster in U.S. history.

Lonnis Bridgeman, Quartus's son, married Artemesia Young of Racine and took over the Syracuse coal and salt business that Quartus started. It was Lonnis who discovered that after salt had been extracted from water, bromine could be made. Lonnis was also a successful superintendent of the Methodist Sunday school in Syracuse, and in later years, he was superintendent of the district of the State Sunday School Union. He died in 1908.

Melinda Bridgeman, known as Lynda, was said to be "very frail all her life." Although she died in 1867 at the age of eighteen, she was said to have loved music and flowers.

The youngest of the Bridgeman six was Quartus Bridgeman IV, who married Jessie McElroy, daughter of Captain J.C. McElroy, and occupied the Bridgeman homestead. His mother remained there until her death. He was identified as having "the best interests of the town and a worker in the Methodist church and Sunday school."

Although Emory never returned home from the Civil War, the branch he stuck in the ground took root and the tree stood at the homestead for more than one hundred years. According to an article in the *Athens Messenger* by Charles H. Harris,

> The village of Syracuse, standing on an eminence over a wide expanse of river bottom land, in the spring resembles a huge bouquet, pink and white and red flowering trees—but one tree in the town has a history that has long been forgotten and is saved but a few to whom it is a community tradition.
>
> One Syracuse tree, not for fruit has withstood the years despite features which do not endear its species to home owners. It is an ailanthus tree, its bloom has an extremely offensive odor and in this instance is the only one in its variety in this area.
>
> The tree has been allowed to stand because it was prized by the family of Quartus Bridgeman, a Meigs County pioneer. It stands at the edge of the sidewalk at the front of the Bridgemans', an extremely patriotic family of early days.

It was for this reason only that the offensive tree, commonly known as the "stink tree," and ironically also known as the tree of heaven, was permitted to stand so long.

In 1891, the same year Rebecca died, the first renovation of the home took place. Ceilings and walls were replastered, then all were painted or wallpapered. The kitchen originally had a large open fireplace with a large iron hook. This was plastered over and a large iron cook stove was put in front of it. Additionally, the cold cellar where milk, butter, eggs and fresh meats were kept was bricked over.

In later years, the Johnson family used the house and a granary and tool house were added to the property. Then a carriage house was added, along with a woodshed, a coalhouse and a henhouse. The property originally held fifteen acres, most of which is hilly and covered in trees. It's also the final resting place of several members of the Bridgeman family.

Before the Houston family purchased the house, it was rented by a Mrs. Capehart. It was during this time that the home became too much to manage and fell into dilapidation.

According to an article by Katie Crow, which appeared in the *Sunday Times-Sentinel* on October 25, 1970, the four generations of the Bridgeman family who owned and occupied the house sold it to Paul and Shirley Houston, who restored it to its "remarkable brilliance."

The restoration undertaken by the Houstons took three years to complete, and Mrs. Houston made all of the curtains and drapes and reupholstered many pieces of antique furniture purchased at auctions. Her late husband, Paul, did all of the brick masonry, plastering, wiring and painting, as well as the installation of nearly 120 panes of glass.

The Civil War tree had fallen into decay and began to go hollow. As fate would have it, the tree was struck by lightning and fell around the same time the Bridgemans sold the estate to the Houstons. One must wonder if the lightning strike was sheer coincidence or the work of the supernatural, symbolizing that the Bridgeman homestead was no longer the property of the Bridgeman family, and the ghost of Emory Bridgeman could no longer return.

The Houstons planted a weeping cherry tree in the same location as the ailanthus tree, and it still stands today. During my visit with Mrs. Shirley Houston, the exterior of the home was receiving a fresh coat of paint and was still one of the most beautiful historic homes of Syracuse. I would like to thank her for allowing me to borrow her book on the Bridgeman family and for sharing the history of her beautiful home.

# Chapter 28

# POMEROY-MIDDLEPORT FOOTBALL RIVALRY

*Rivalry: (noun) competition for the same objective or for superiority in the same field.*

T he most active rivalry in Meigs County today would have be between the Southern Tornadoes and the Eastern Eagles. The last football game of the regular season is played on a Saturday night, either at Roger Lee Adams Field in Racine or at East Shade River Stadium in Reedsville and has come to be named the "Battle for the Boot" because of the boot shape of the Ohio River that encompasses the Southern and Eastern school districts.

But there is another rivalry that dates back way before than that of the Tornadoes and Eagles. All you have to do is dust off the old yearbooks of the Pomeroy Panthers and the Middleport Yellow Jackets to see what was one of the fiercest football rivalries in the state of Ohio.

A 1926 edition of the *Pomeroyan* stated,

> The reintroduction of football this year as an official sport of P.H.S. was hailed with delight by the local fans. To Coach Samson goes most of the credit for it was largely through his efforts that football is now allowed. One of the chief objections to the game was the cost of equipment. This was overcame [*sic*] when the businessmen of Pomeroy contributed enough money to pay a large part of the expense. Not only the business men, but a great many others helped pay for the equipment. THANKS to all who did. THE TEAM.

During the first year football was reintroduced, Pomeroy played the Middleport Scouts—presumably the reserve team—twice. In the first game on the schedule, the Scouts beat the Panthers by a score of thirteen to zero. Pomeroy lost the next two games, first to Cheshire by a score of thirty to zero and then to Rutland twenty-four to zero. Week four was a rematch for the Panthers and the Scouts. This time the Panthers walked away with their first win that season. The next game, the Panthers won on a forfeit from Cheshire, and the recorded score for the game was one to zero. In the final game of the season, the Panthers and the Yellow Jackets met on November 26, 1925, Thanksgiving Day, and the actual Yellow Jackets walked away with the victory with a final score of forty to twelve. This began what would be a forty-two-year rivalry between the Middleport Yellow Jackets and the Pomeroy Panthers.

In that same 1925–26 school year, Pomeroy High School joined the newly formed Southeastern Ohio Athletic League (SEOAL). The Jackson Ironmen, Logan Chieftains, Athens Bulldogs, Gallia Academy Blue Devils, Ironton Fighting Tigers, Nelsonville Greyhounds, Portsmouth Trojans and Wellston Golden Rockets were charter members of what would go on to be Ohio's oldest noncity athletic league, which dissolved ninety-two years later, in 2017. The Pomeroy Panthers joined a few months after the league was formed. The Middleport Yellow Jackets joined in 1929 and went on to be a dominating factor in the SEOAL for the next twelve years. Both the Panthers and Yellow Jackets remained in the league until the Meigs High School consolidation in 1967, when both schools were combined with the Rutland Red Devils. The Meigs Marauders remained in the SEOAL until 1983, when they made the move to their current Tri-Valley Conference, where they are in the Ohio Division.

Interestingly enough, Middleport and Pomeroy both played all of their home games at Middleport's Pythian Park from 1926 until Yellow Jacket Stadium was built by the Works Progress Administration (WPA) in 1935. Yellow Jacket Stadium is one of eighty stadiums in Ohio that were either built or completed by the WPA. Pomeroy residents went to the polls on November 4, 1941, and approved a bond issue for the development of a stadium. This included grading the site and erecting the steel stadium, ticket office and necessary fencing. In fall of 1950, the Panthers took their own home field in week three against Wellston and defeated the Golden Rockets with a score of twelve to zero. That Thanksgiving, the Panthers traveled to the familiar territory of Yellow Jacket Stadium where the Yellow Jackets won with a score of thirty-three to twelve.

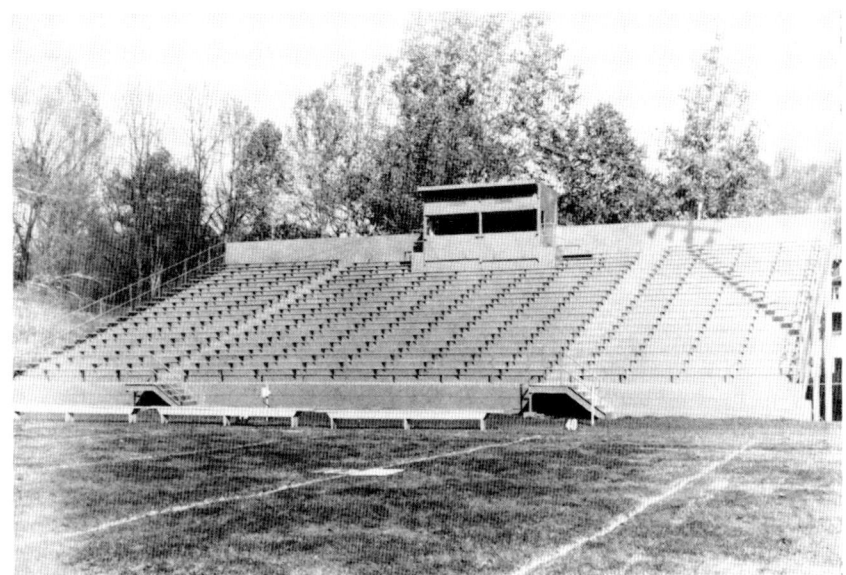

POMEROY FOOTBALL STADIUM

Pomeroy Football Stadium was home of the Pomeroy Panthers until the consolidation of Pomeroy, Middleport and Rutland High Schools into Meigs High School. It was used by the Marauders on Friday nights until the opening of Farmers Bank Stadium behind Meigs High School. *From author's collection.*

On Thanksgiving in 1951, the Yellow Jackets traveled to the new home of the Pomeroy Panthers. According to a 1952 edition of the *Pomeroyan*, "The frozen field thawed on Thanksgiving making it a sea of mud. The Jackets scored in the first quarter, but the attempted conversion was blocked…. Pomeroy's defense just wasn't clicking and the Jackets scored again in on a pass in the final quarter. The gun sounded and the game ended 12–0."

The last time these rivals met on Thanksgiving was in 1959. The Yellow Jackets headed to Pomeroy to take on the Panthers. The Panthers won that day with a score of fourteen to eight. Seven years later, in the fall of 1966, the Panthers and the Yellow Jackets faced off one final time. The final score was Pomeroy thirty-two, Middleport sixteen. Of the forty-two games played, Middleport won nineteen and Pomeroy won eighteen. Five games ended in a tie. The scores of all forty-two games:

1925: Middleport 40, Pomeroy 12
1926: Middleport 19, Pomeroy 0
1927: Middleport 6, Pomeroy 0

1928: Middleport 19, Pomeroy 0
1929: Middleport 38, Pomeroy 0
1930: Middleport 45, Pomeroy 0
1931: Middleport 0, Pomeroy 0 (TIE)
1932: Pomeroy 25, Middleport 0 (First Pomeroy Win)
1933: Middleport 6, Pomeroy 0
1934: Middleport 12, Pomeroy 6
1935: Middleport 19, Pomeroy 0
1936: Pomeroy 18, Middleport 6
1937: Pomeroy 39, Middleport 0
1938: Middleport 0, Pomeroy 0 (TIE)
1939: Middleport 0, Pomeroy 0 (TIE)
1940: Pomeroy 20, Middleport 12
1941: Pomeroy 20, Middleport 0
1942: Middleport 7, Pomeroy 6
1943: Middleport 13, Pomeroy 13 (TIE)
1944: Middleport 0, Pomeroy 0
1945: Middleport 20, Pomeroy 12
1946: Pomeroy 12, Middleport 7
1947: Middleport 12, Pomeroy 6
1948: Pomeroy 7, Middleport 6
1949: Middleport 13, Pomeroy 13 (TIE)
1950: Middleport 33, Pomeroy 12
1951: Middleport 12, Pomeroy 0 (First game on Pomeroy's field)
1952: Middleport 57, Pomeroy 0
1953: Middleport 26, Pomeroy 13
1954: Pomeroy 38, Middleport 0
1955: Pomeroy 53, Middleport 0
1956: Pomeroy 34, Middleport 13
1957: Pomeroy 27, Middleport 0
1958: Pomeroy 44, Middleport 12
1959: Pomeroy 14, Middleport 8 (Last game on Thanksgiving Day)
1960: Middleport 18, Pomeroy 14
1961: Pomeroy 60, Middleport 14
1962: Pomeroy 14, Middleport 6
1963: Pomeroy 32, Middleport 8
1964: Pomeroy 18, Middleport 14
1965: Middleport 6, Pomeroy 0
1966: Pomeroy 32, Middleport 16

Roscoe "Sonny" Wise and his wife, Mary, remarked, "We don't remember Thanksgiving dinner…just the game." Today, the Thanksgiving rivalry lives on when former Yellow Jackets and Panthers alike gather at Yellow Jackets Stadium for what has come to be known as the "Meeting of the Ghosts." They share stories of former glory days and keep this once-fierce rivalry alive with a coin toss to determine the winner of the year's game.

# Chapter 29

# POMEROY BEND BRIDGE

O n November 12, 1928, the Pomeroy Bend Bridge, or as it came to be known, the Pomeroy-Mason Bridge, opened to traffic and would serve the people of Meigs County, Ohio, and Mason County, West Virginia, until January 31, 2009. But this bridge served much more than the people of these respective counties: it connected the large cities of the north and the south, opened opportunity for growth and required military enforcement for crowd control during its opening. Our bridge of the past was once a bridge of the future.

While the bridge was built and opened in 1928, its origins date back as early as 1914 with W.A. Compton and W.F. Reed filling leadership roles in promoting a joint bridge and highway project. Compton and Reed garnered support from the Ohio towns through which the proposed highway would run. Support eventually led to interest in West Virginia, which led to the passage of the Good Roads Amendment on November 2, 1920. This allotted more than $85 million in West Virginia state bonds to finance the construction and maintenance of a state road system that would connect the various county seats.

During Compton and Reed's tenure promoting U.S. 33 and the Pomeroy Bend Bridge, the pair was contacted by Ralph and Frank Dravo from the Dravo Contracting Company of Pittsburgh, leading to final plans for the construction of a bridge. This million-dollar bridge would have a cantilever span of 1,185 feet, a channel span of 665 feet and a road length just shy of a half mile. The steel structure would measure 1847.75 feet on four concrete

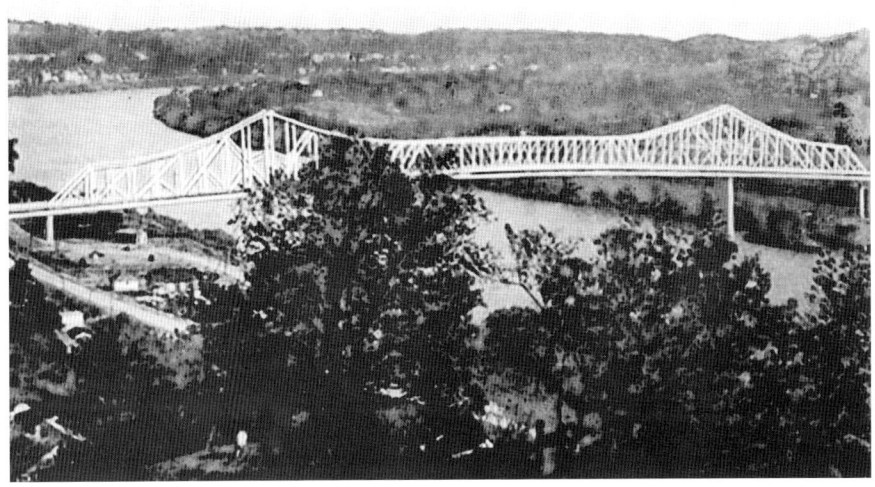

This postcard shows the Pomeroy Bend Bridge, commonly known as the Pomeroy-Mason Bridge, looking upriver from Flood Road. *From author's collection.*

piers and the height from the center span to the river would be 97 feet. It was constructed by Mount Vernon Bridge Company of Mount Vernon, Ohio. The bridge was originally owned by the Pomeroy-Mason Bridge Company, a subsidiary of Dravo Contracting Company. In 1939, the State of Ohio acquired ownership of the bridge.

After the concrete piers were poured, the first steel was placed in June 1928, and the steel structures on both sides of the river were connected in the center on August 22, 1928. According to Ervin's *Pioneer History of Meigs County*, "The masonry and concrete work took eight months, and the painting and general conditioning after the steel work was finished required two months, making just a year in the complete erecting of the imposing structure…just two months after the first steel was laid, making a record for Ohio River bridge building…conceded to be the Ohio Valley's finest bridge."

According to the November 11, 1928 issue of the *Athens Messenger*, "60 National Guardsmen under the command of Capt. Harry Bennett will keep the avenues of communication open and cars moving throughout the day." To accommodate the huge influx of spectators from all over the region, cars were forbidden to park along Second Street in Pomeroy. This was enforced with "military precision" to allow delegates to stage for the opening ceremonies. The bridge was opened to allow spectators to find

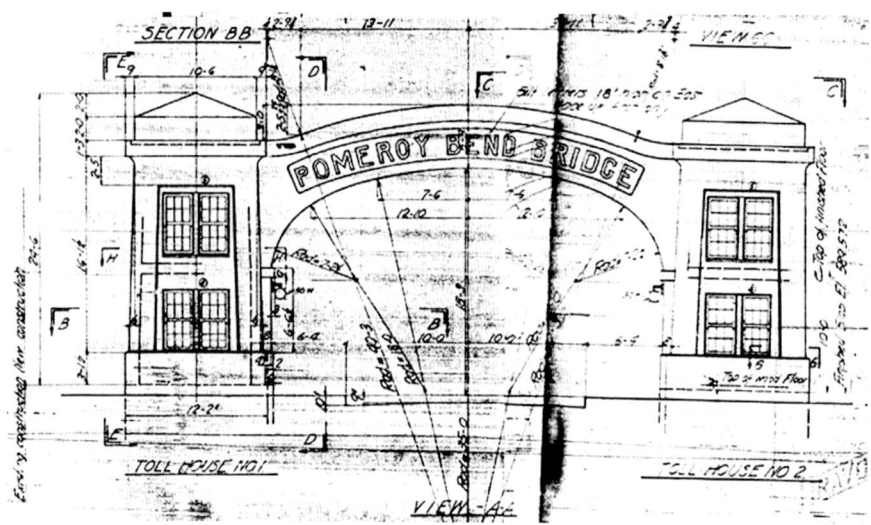

Blueprints of the Pomeroy Bend Bridge and Tollhouse. *From author's collection.*

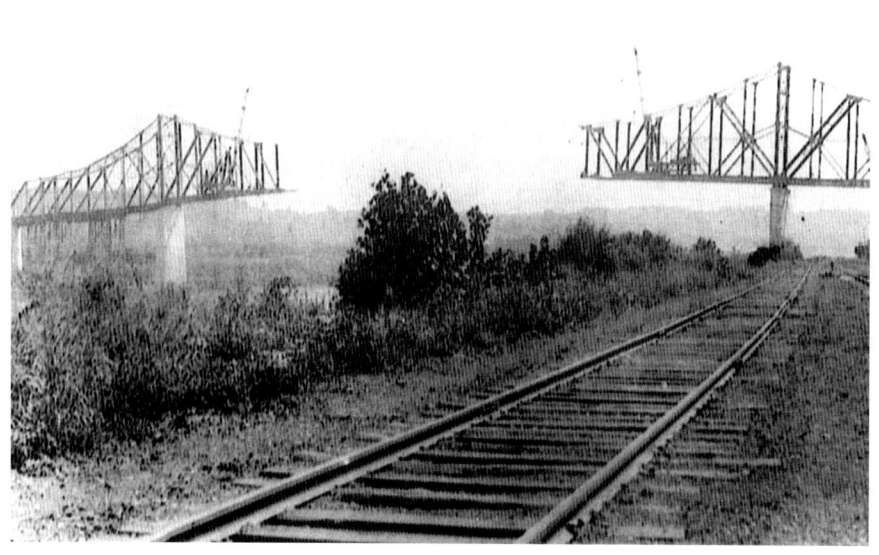

The Pomeroy Bend Bridge under construction in 1928. The bridge connected Columbus, Ohio, to Charleston, West Virginia, as part of US 33, also known as the Blue and Gray Trail. *From author's collection.*

ample parking in the vacant lots and the broad streets of Mason City, West Virginia. This was overseen by troopers of the West Virginia State Police.

A delegation traveled the length of the new U.S. Route 33 Blue and Gray Trail from Columbus, Ohio, to Ripley, West Virginia, to mark the historic occasion of the opening of the bridge. Ohio governor A. Victor Donahey, West Virginia governor Howard M. Gore and U.S. senator Simeon D. Fess, as well as other distinguished guests, spoke at the opening of the Pomeroy Bend Bridge. Spectators filled the bridge and the vacant lots on both sides of the bridge to take part in the opening ceremonies. Before and after the ceremony, the bridge was opened toll free for its first day of traffic.

The Pomeroy Bend Bridge was said to connect the principal cites of Ohio, Michigan, West Virginia, Virginia and North Carolina. Pomeroy served as a "hub of a gigantic wheel of good roads to a commercial betterment of the city by direct routes meeting here throughout Ohio." The Pomeroy Bend Bridge linked the Great Lakes to the tidewaters of Virginia and was the terminus connecting Detroit, Michigan, to Miami, Florida.

The Pomeroy Bend Bridge replaced the *Champion No. 3* ferryboat in 1928. After the bridge opened, the former Pomeroy-Mason ferry served as a ferryboat in Proctorville, Ohio. The same year the Pomeroy Bend Bridge opened to traffic, the Silver Bridge opened downriver, connecting Gallipolis, Ohio, and Point Pleasant, West Virginia. The Pomeroy Bend Bridge stopped charging a toll in 1949, and the toll houses on the West Virginia side of the bridge were demolished. The bridge underwent major restoration in 1976, and another ferryboat was brought in for the duration of the construction.

The bridge continued to serve as the US 33 connector until 2003, when the U.S. 33 relocation in Meigs County was completed, and the U.S. 33 designation was moved onto the William S. Ritchie Jr. Bridge connecting Portland, Ohio, and Ravenswood, West Virginia. The Pomeroy Bend Bridge was demolished at 8:49 a.m. on April 21, 2009, after eighty years of service. The Ohio pier plaque is in the archives of the Meigs County Historical Society and the West Virginia pier plaque is in the archives of the Point Pleasant River Museum.

# Chapter 30

# EARLY SALT MINING HISTORY IN THE OHIO VALLEY

T he following is an extract from *The Pioneer History of Meigs County* by Stillman Carter Larkin.

In giving an account of this indispensable article I will introduce an extract from the life of Griffin Green, by S.P. Hildreth. "In 1794, when salt was worth from $6 to $8 a bushel, he projected an expedition into the Indian country near the Scioto river for the discovery of the salt springs said to be worked by the savages near the present town of Jackson. At the hazard of his life and all those with him, ten or twelve in number, he succeeded in finding the saline water and boiled some of it down on the spot in their camp kettle, making about a tablespoonful of salt. While here he narrowly escaped death from the rifle of an Indian who discovered them, unobserved by the party. After peace was concluded, this warrior related the circumstance of his raising his rifle twice to fire at a tall man who had a tin cup strung to his girdle on his loins and who was known to be Mr. Green. As he might miss his object, being a long shot, and be killed himself, he desisted and hurried back to the Indian village below the present town of Chillicothe for aid. A party of twenty warriors turned out in pursuit and came on to the bank of the Ohio at Leading creek a few minutes after the whites had left it with their boat and were in the middle of the river. They were seen by the men in the boat, who felt how narrowly and providentially they had escaped."

The first settlers here got their salt from these Scioto salt works. The writer remembers hearing his father tell of taking a horse and pack saddle and going to the "Scioto Licks," as they were then called, and working a week for a sack of salt. His business was drawing saltwater by means of a hand pole affixed to a sweep above. After receiving his wages, put his salt on the pack saddle and made his way home. Those salt works were under the superintendency of a state officer, and by a law passed January 24th, 1804, renters had to pay a tax of 4 cents per gallon on the capacity of the kettle used in making salt, provided always that no person or company shall under any pretense whatever be permitted to use at any time a greater number of kettles or vessels than will contain 4000 gallons, nor a less number in any one furnace than 600 gallons. After the salt works on the Kanawha were started the people here depended on Kanawha for salt, and for many years it was a place of considerable trade. Young men, on coming of age, went to Kanawha to chop wood or tend kettles when they wished to obtain a little money. It was hardly expected to get money at any other place, and salt seemed to be the medium by which trade was conducted.

Keelboats were used as a means of transportation, and shipments were made by them of salt to Marietta, Pittsburg and the lower Ohio. In order to give some knowledge of the origin and progress of the Kanawha salt business, we append a letter which appeared in the Niles Register, Baltimore, Md., in April, 1815, and we copy from the Meigs County Telegraph, April, 1884.

Kanawha Salt Works.
At the first settlement of this place there was a great "buffalo lick," as it was called, was discovered where some weak salt water oozed out of the bank of the river. After some time the inhabitants sunk hollow gums into the sand and gravel at that place, into which the water collected, but it was so weak that, although sufficient quantities might be collected, not more than two to four bushels were made in a day. After the property came into the possession of my brother, Joseph Ruffner, and myself (by divisee), we were desirous to see the effect of sinking large sycamore gums as low down as we could force them. We found great difficulty in this on account of the water coming in so rapidly. When we got down about eighteen feet below the surface of the river we discovered that our gums lodged on a solid, smooth freestone rock, and the water was but little improved as we descended. We then bored a hole in the rock

about 2 1/2 inches in diameter, the size generally used subsequently for that purpose. After penetrating the rock eighteen or twenty feet, we struck a vein of water saltier than had been attained in this place before. Our neighbors followed our example and succeeded in obtaining good saltwater in the distance of 2 1/2 miles below and four miles above us on the river. They all have to sink the gums about eighteen feet to the rock, into which they bore a hole from 100 to 200 feet deep. The rock is never perforated, though the water seeps into the holes in soft or porous places. The cost of boring was from $3 to $4 a foot. The first water that is struck in the augur hole is fresh, or an inferior quality of salt water, which is excluded by means of copper or tin tubes put down into the augur hole and secured so that none of the water that comes in above the lower end of the tube can discharge itself into the gum, which has a bottom put into it immediately upon the rock, and is secured in such a manner that no water can get into the tube except that which comes up through the tube from below. The water thus gathered in the gum rises about as high as the surface of the river at high water mark, and it requires from seventy to 100 gallons of it to make a bushel of salt. Each well produced on an average a sufficient quantity of water to make 300 bushels of salt per day. There are now established and in operation fifty-two furnaces, and more are being erected, containing from forty to sixty kettles of thirty-five gallons each, which make from 2500 to 3000 bushels of salt per day. The quantity may be increased as the demand shall justify. The wood in the course of time must become scarce or difficult to obtain, but we have stone coal that can be used for fuel, and the supply is inexhaustible. These works are situated six miles above Charleston, Kanawha Courthouse, sixty-six miles from the mouth of the river and twenty-six miles below the great falls. The river is navigable, with a gentle current, at all seasons of the year for boats drawing two feet of water, and at most seasons for boats of any size.

Your obedient, humble servant, David Ruffner.
Kanawha Salt Works, November 8th, 1814.

It appears from old account books that salt rated as high as $2 per bushel in Rutland township as late as 1820. The first saltwater seen on Leading creek was a small pond of reddish water, which in dry weather cattle would visit for drink, the place being near the channel of the creek, about a quarter of a mile below the old Denny mill, in a bend of Leading creek. In 1820 several of the neighbors brought in their kettles and set them on a kind of furnace and made of that water one bushel of salt. After which a company was formed consisting of Benjamin Stout, Caleb Gardner, Thomas Shepherd and Michael Aleshire, who bored a well and erected a furnace and commenced making salt in 1822, when Benjamin Stout bought out the other parties.

In 1822 Abijah Hubbell and his son, Jabez Hubbell, and Barsley Hubbell bored a salt well above the Stout well and a furnace set for making salt in 1824.

Ruel Braley manufactured salt at his works, five miles above on Leading creek, in 1830.

The Bradford and Stedman's furnace was located about five miles below the Stout well in 1830 or 1831.

Still further down the creek Theophilus Jacobs operated a furnace for a few years with a great deal of energy.

Near the mouth of Thomas Fork Herriman Plummer bored a well and made salt in 1831.

Two other salt wells had been previously attempted in Rutland township, but failed to obtain saltwater. One was bored by Joseph Giles, Sr., and the other one was by Samuel Church in 1822, which resulted in the discovery of a heavy lubricating oil, the true value of which was not understood and very little attention was paid to it.

After the Rutland furnaces began to make 200 bushels of salt per week the prices came down to 50 cents a bushel. After salt was made in large quantities along the Ohio river the works on the creek became unprofitable, and the manufacture of salt was discontinued.

# ABOUT THE AUTHORS

*J*ordan D. Pickens and his wife, Calee, have been married since 2013 and are lifelong residents of Meigs County. Jordan previously released *Images of America: Meigs County*, which he coauthored with Dr. Ivan M. Tribe. He was an associate producer for the Emmy-nominated *Our Town: Pomeroy* documentary, under Evan Shaw. Jordan and Calee are both former trustees of the Meigs County Pioneer and Historical Society, where Jordan served as president and Calee as museum director. Jordan teaches social studies at Southern High School, and Calee teaches science at Meigs Middle School. They have two children, Andrew and Clara.

*Visit us at*
www.historypress.com